WHAT THE CHAMPIONS SAY ABOUT JACK LE GOFF

"In my 60 years in the horse business, I have assigned the word 'genius' to very few men or women. Jack was one of those rare few. He had it all. He had enormous natural talent as a rider, teacher, and trainer. Jack was one of the few remaining men who had a thorough education in the classic French school, one of the great schools in the history of riding. Jack himself rode in the Olympic Games, and his record as a coach at the international and Olympic level is unsurpassed possibly by any equestrian discipline. Across the board, as a rider, teacher, trainer, coach, judge, and now author, Jack Le Goff gets my vote as number one!"

George H. Morris
Former Chef d'Equipe US Show Jumping Team

"The most successful equestrian coach in history finally allows us a unique look behind the scene. Jack Le Goff was a genius, and any horseman will want this book, not just for what you will learn about training horses, but about the internal qualities that set Jack apart, and turned him into a legend."

Jim Wofford
Three-Time Olympian

"Jack Le Goff gave a new meaning to the saying 'a legend in his lifetime' and to what we mean as an 'icon in the sport.' Very few people achieve as much as Jack did during his lifetime. I count myself fortunate to have known him as a friend and to have been able to benefit from the knowledge of a truly remarkable horseman."

Captain Mark Phillips
Former Chef d'Equipe US Eventing Team

"I am a product of what Jack Le Goff taught me; I spent 17 years working with Jack, and you don't forget that. He was a good friend and an even greater horseman, and I have the highest regard and respect for the man. Whenever any of us would have some disagreement with him he would say, 'Whatever problems we have we are going to resolve them and come away from this as friends.' And we did. I learned to my cost the value of not listening to him (as I know he tells you in this book). The times I made mistakes on course were the times I didn't listen. When I did listen, I was successful. Jack was an amazing teacher.

"I have been told by many people that I could write a book about what I have done, and I have to say that out of 30 chapters, 20 would be about Jack. Whether I am teaching or riding, Jack is always there with me. His words and his teaching are in my head and always will be. You have to appreciate this man. If people do not, and cannot, learn anything from his book, then they should not be eventing."

J. Michael Plumb
Olympic Gold Medalist,
First Equestrian Inductee US Olympic Hall of Fame

"One of my greatest gifts of good fortune was to be a young rider with Jack Le Goff. A genius on a horse, I remember being mesmerized by his abilities to transform a horse. He understood, perhaps better than anyone, the physical and mental needs, abilities, and limitations of this noble creature. Jack had a brilliant mind. He thought about and cared deeply for the horse and for the future of all equestrian sports. As both a student and a master of the game, he dedicated his life and energies to the future well-being of both and to the education of those of us who share his interests. He set the example and the standard for all of us to follow. Jack was a gifted teacher, trainer, and coach. His language abilities and understanding of human nature enabled him to impart his education, skill, and expertise to so many of us over the years. More importantly, his lessons and insights were part of a larger philosophy of riding, horsemanship, and life that have guided me and others through the years."

Tad Coffin
Olympic Gold Medalist

"When Jack Le Goff was appointed as Chef d'Equipe for, what was then the USET Three-Day Eventing Squad, he single-handedly revolutionized the sport in the United States. He became a true ambassador for eventing in America, taking us from a group of local, loosely organized competitors to a force to be reckoned with on the international scene. The opportunity to work under Jack on a daily basis was the highlight of my equestrian education. He was classically trained and a rigorous taskmaster, but more importantly, he possessed the uncanny ability to customize his training methods to each horse and rider. He enhanced our strong points and, after explicitly describing our faults to all within earshot, proceeded to show us how to turn these weaknesses into strengths. For this, we are forever grateful! I will always admire Jack for his sixth sense with the horses and his unique ability to leave the lessons of the day in the barn. This allowed us all to enjoy Jack's wit and charm and maintain a friendly bond 'after hours.' For these reasons and countless more, Jack will forever stand as my eventing mentor."

Karen Stives
Olympic Gold Medalist

"After considering all of the extraordinary strengths and accomplishments of this man, what stands out the most about Jack Le Goff is what an incredible horseman he was—a very rare breed then and even more so later. Jack truly loved and cherished his horses. He was instinctive about their strengths and needs. His coaching was invaluable, and his knowledge and consideration of the horses in his trust were unprecedented. How privileged I was to ride the finest horse in the world and be coached by the finest horseman."

Torrance Watkins
Olympic Gold Medalist

HORSES CAME FIRST, SECOND, AND LAST

My Unapologetic Road to Eventing Gold

Jack Le Goff

with Jo Whitehouse

TRAFALGAR SQUARE
North Pomfret, Vermont

First published in 2017 by
Trafalgar Square Books
North Pomfret, Vermont 05053

DISCLAIMER OF LIABILITY

LIBRARY OF CONGRESS CATALOGING-IN-PUBLICATION DATA
Names: Le Goff, Jack, 1931-2009, author. | Whitehouse, Jo, author.
Title: Horses came first, second and last : my unapologetic road to eventing
   gold / Jack Le Goff with Jo Whitehouse ; foreword by David O'Connor.
Description: North Pomfret, Vermont : Trafalgar Square Books, 2017. |
   Includes index.
Identifiers: LCCN 2017026485 (print) | LCCN 2017034029 (ebook) | ISBN
   9781570768682 (epub) | ISBN 9781570768279 (paperback)
Subjects: LCSH: Le Goff, Jack, 1931-2009. | Eventing (Horsemanship)--United
   States--Biography. | Horsemanship--Coaching--United States--Biography. |
   BISAC: SPORTS & RECREATION / Equestrian. | BIOGRAPHY & AUTOBIOGRAPHY /
   Sports. | PETS / Horses / General.
Classification: LCC SF295.7 (ebook) | LCC SF295.7 .L42 2017 (print) | DDC
   798.2092 [B] --dc23
LC record available at https://lccn.loc.gov/2017026485

Main cover photograph by Susan Smith; insets (top to bottom) courtesy of Jack Le Goff; by Alix Coleman; by Fifi Coles. Back cover photo by Fifi Coles.
Book design by DOQ
Cover design by RM Didier
Typeface: Fira Sans
Printed in the United States of America
10 9 8 7 6 5 4 3 2

This book is dedicated to my family. Their constant support, particularly during the inevitable tough times, has allowed me to fulfill my dreams.

My deepest gratitude is a small thank you compared to all the sacrifices my family has endured with such grace and selflessness.

A Note from the Publisher

Jack Le Goff
1931–2009

These pages reflect his life until he
completed this book in 2005.

CONTENTS

PREFACE

As I approach the retirement years, many questions cross my mind. How will I cope without being involved in top class competitions all over the world? Will I miss seeing my friends, my colleagues? Perhaps they will keep in touch with me. Will I miss the hustle and bustle of the Olympic Games and the exhilaration and thrill of being part of one of the most exciting gatherings of so many different people of the world? I don't know! Could I attend the Olympics as a spectator? Undoubtedly I could, but I do not think I want to. Having being intensely involved in 11 Olympic Games, I don't think I would enjoy just being a spectator with no access to the action; to the horses, the riders, the officials.

Will I miss the horses, the riders, the teaching? Likely so. Helping a raw young horse learn and discover what he can do, what he is capable of, and taking that horse to the highest level of competition is one of the most satisfying things one can do. I will miss my involvement in the development of young riders like the Jean-Jacques Guyons, the Tad Coffins, the Bruce Davidsons, the David O'Connors, helping them to get to the top of the international scene. Perhaps in the writing of this book and sharing the things learned over the last 50 years in the sport I will find some answers.

More than anything, my life has been one of a horseman above all else. Horses came first, second, and last, to the point where I likely sacrificed too much of my family for them.

This book is about the things learned throughout my life as a horse-man, not only about training horses and riders, but also about the diversity of people met and how to deal with the different person-alities that are an integral part of the sport, the owners, the orga-nizers, the media, to mention a few. So my purpose is to transmit to aspiring riders, and anyone who has an interest in equestrian sports, what I have learned throughout the different phases of my life, and will include some specific technical aspects of dressage, conditioning, cross-country and show jumping.

The writing of this book presents the perfect opportunity to rec-ognize some of the people who had a profound influence on my life and career. My father was my first teacher and had an indeli-ble impact at the beginning of my riding career. I had an immense admiration for him. Like a lot of his contemporaries in those days, he was an all-around horseman who could train a Grand Prix dres-sage horse, a Grand Prix show jumper, and at the same time, train and ride racehorses. Unfortunately, the opportunity to learn so much more from him ended when he had a fatal accident in a stee-plechase at the young age of 41 years.

Later I was lucky enough to work with exceptional people like Col-onel George Margot, Chief Ecuyer of the Cadre Noir, who taught me probably 90 percent of what I know about dressage. Captain Ber-nard de Fombelle was a very successful international show jumping rider, well known for his genius in riding and training show jumpers as well as his unorthodox and intriguing personality. We spent two years together in the same squadron in a mounted regiment during the Algerian war. When not engaged in military operations we had an agreement where he would help me with show jumping, and I would help him with dressage. That was a very remarkable and educational experience!

It was my great fortune to be at Gladstone for four years when Bert de Némethy was the trainer, coach, and chef d'equipe of the show jumping team. We shared the same office and the ring. In observing Bert ride and train the team I had the chance to appreciate his very systematic and consistent schooling and preparation of show jumping horses and riders. Bert being undoubtedly one of the most respected jumping coaches in history, it was for me a golden opportunity. We also had some interesting exchanges on riding in general, and we cooperated in assisting each other with the horses.

Looking back at my career it was hard work, and at times very hard work. Being a lot older now I sometimes wonder how I found the energy and the time to accomplish all those things, but it was fascinating to me.

And I had fun doing it.

Jack Le Goff
Saumur, 2005

ACKNOWLEDGMENTS

A great thank you to Jo Whitehouse for her enthusiastic support in the writing of this book. Jo found the time in her busy schedule to do the hours of research necessary to report the historical facts accurately and to translate numerous tapes into the written word. Her positive attitude all along the road to the finished product has been a great help to me.

I would also like to give a special thank you to Mary Miller, a brilliant mind and a sharp lawyer who has used her editing talents to ensure the manuscript was well organized, coordinated, and coherent. Often, we horse people speak in a language not immediately understood by those who are new to equestrian sports. Mary showed us where more explanation was needed and constantly kept us on track. She is a very special friend, and I truly appreciate and value all her advice and assistance.

My deepest appreciation goes wholeheartedly to the exceptionally wonderful ground personnel who have made my job possible over the years. The grooms, stable and farm managers who have been so dedicated and totally devoted to the horses and the Team. I cannot sufficiently express my sincere gratitude to all of them. They spend most of the time in the shadows, but they are the most important link between the horses, the riders and the coach in the success of a team.

Thank you, my friends!

PART I

THE LEARNING YEARS

"Since I was not born with the
wealth I deserved."

1

TWENTY KILOS IS ALL!

But for my father I might have lived my life as a country farmer in the French countryside of Brittany. Louis Le Goff was born in 1907, to a Breton family in a farming community in western France. Most families in the area were farmers who dabbled in a little bit of everything: cattle, pigs, corn, rabbits, chickens, and vegetables. My grandparents kept one or two broodmares and bred horses to sell to the army. This was before the time of mechanical farming and horses were used for everything from plowing the fields to pulling the hay wagons to taking the family to church every Sunday in the carriage. As a young boy, my father helped on the farm every day and was especially keen on raising and training the young horses and presenting them for sale to prospective buyers. This was the part that he loved the most and no hour spent with a horse was a wasted hour as far as he was concerned.

At that time in France, military service was compulsory and, at 20 years of age, my father went willingly as the branch of service he entered was the cavalry, which meant he could continue to be around horses. The cavalry held or participated in numerous equestrian competitions but to qualify you had to be at the very least a non-commissioned officer. True to his nature, my father applied himself to that aspect of his life as he did everything else, with energy and enthusiasm and was quickly rewarded with a promotion to the rank of Marechal des Logis (sergeant). The types of competitions available were many and varied, but it was show jumping and steeplechasing at which my father excelled. In Europe, steeplechase racing is as important as flat racing, much more so than in the United States and the race meets are held on the commercial racetracks. At a regular meet there often were a total of eight races, two of which would be military races. One of these would be for non-commissioned officers and one for the officers. To enter the officers' race the horses had to have won three non-commissioned officers' races, otherwise they were not allowed to run. My father was a small man and a superb rider, so everyone wanted him to ride their horses to qualify them for the officers' races. Every week he had his pick of any number of horses to ride and was very successful—all of which led him to not want to return home to the farm after his period of military service ended. He stayed in the French army for the sake of the horses and no other reason. This was a life-changing decision and one that affected not only his life but the lives of his future children.

Louis Le Goff was now a career army man in the French Cavalry and would work his way up the ladder to fully fledged officer. Shortly after this he met and married my mother Marie-Ange and in 1931 I was born in Normandy where my father was stationed.

In 1936, my father had a chance to attend the Cadre Noir in Saumur and at the same time was given the opportunity to go to Tunisia, then a protectorate of France, to be on the staff of the Bey Guard (the equivalent of the Horse Guards in Britain). While he had always intended to make the Cadre Noir his goal, my father felt he could do that later, and elected to go to Tunis where, when not involved in official duties, he played a lot of polo, rode racehorses and show jumpers, and had a whale of a time. He developed a deep interest in the native Barb horses and the Arab/Barb crosses, especially since there were races specifically for the Arab horses, run under French racing rules and in which my father avidly took part. There is no doubt that his years in the army were the best of his life—in fact, I think that was the best time of all of our lives, including my mother and me. We lived in the city of Tunis where my father's position in the army entitled us to a lovely house that included two stalls for the horses. Mother had a *fatma*, a woman who served as a maid to the household and it was here that my little brother Pierre was born.

The Bey Guard was headquartered quite close, and Father would ride his horses in the morning to keep them conditioned and then fulfill his commitments as an army officer. He played polo for North Africa for a while and used some Arab horses and some Arabs with a little Barb in them, which made them very sturdy, clever, and extremely fast. He also enjoyed gliding. Gliding, known as "soaring" in the United States, has universal appeal. Gliding or soaring is motor-less flight, using a sailplane and natural occurring atmospheric phenomena, called "LIFT," to gain altitude and stay aloft. Gliders, or more correctly, sailplanes are often described as motorless airplanes and were used extensively in World War II to transport troops and equipment silently behind enemy lines.

THE WAR

But in 1939, this enjoyable life came to an end with the outbreak of World War II in Europe. The family did not return to France and my father never got to fulfill his dream of the Cadre Noir.

France was occupied by the German army of Adolph Hitler. Interestingly enough, in the peace accord between the Germans and Mussolini (the Italians were allied with the Germans) there was a clause that the North African French Army, meaning Tunisia, Algeria, and Morocco, would remain neutral and would not take sides and fight against the Germans or the Italians.

The armistice accord signed by the Germans and the French Vichy government allowed for a very limited number of officers to be stationed there, which was much fewer than the number of officers that in fact existed. To comply with these restrictions, the French disguised the commissioned officers as warrant officers so that they could remain in North Africa. Of course, it was understood by all that as soon as the war was over the officers would return to their original ranks. The Germans did not occupy Tunisia, but would spot check from time to time to see that the accord was being respected.

We continued to live in Tunis rather than return to France, and there was a great deal of sadness upon hearing that all our furniture and possessions there had been stolen or burned during the German occupation. We never did know precisely what happened, and life was extremely hard throughout this time, but at least the family was together.

In 1943, father was transferred to Meknes in Morocco and on the way we stopped overnight in Algiers. The city of Algiers reminds me of San Francisco; it is a lovely city which sits on a hill overlooking the bay. We were wakened in the middle of the night by gunshots and tracing bullets seemed to be flying everywhere. Tracing bullets have lights and bear a close resemblance to fireworks which to a 12-year-old was pretty exciting and made such an impression I still remember the scene vividly to this day. At daybreak, we were amazed to see the bay filled with American warships bunched very tightly together. Each ship had a cable attached to a balloon flying high in the air, and I found out that this was to prevent the German planes diving on the ships and firing on the crews. There was no way they could get close enough without getting tangled in the cables. American soldiers were out in their GMC trucks throwing chewing gum at the children who had no idea what it was having never seen it before. Father wondered what on earth had happened so went to the military headquarters to find out. He was told that the Americans had just landed. No one knew that they were supposed to land that night and the local military thought they were being invaded so fired some warning shots. All that stopped when they realized it was the US Army and the people were then very welcoming to the US soldiers. Father was told to keep going to Morocco and join his unit there, which he dutifully did.

In Morocco, my father was assigned to the 5th Spahis Mounted Regiment of Morocco, which was made up of 90 percent native Moroccans. Strangely enough, the regiment was sent back to Tunisia from where my father had just traveled. The cavalry soldiers joked that they and their horses were going to stop Rommel and his tanks coming up from Libya. Fortunately for them, Rommel had already been stopped by British troops under General Montgomery. Mother, my brother Pierre, and I stayed in Meknes with a very harsh time ahead of us.

From 1943 to the end of the war, my father's regiment spent almost three years traveling on horseback from Tunisia to Italy, back through France and then north to land in Germany. The North African Army had joined forces with the British and Americans to fight the Germans and two North African Spahis regiments served on horseback throughout World War II: my father's—the 5th Regiment of Spahis, and an Algerian Spahis Regiment. Today it might sound a little outdated but it was the way of strategic warfare then. Riders were sent out on reconnaissance ahead of the armored divisions to report what they found. This meant the tanks did not have to expose themselves until they knew what was ahead and it worked very well. During the recent conflict with Afghanistan it was suggested that the US Army consider using horses once again because the arid, mountainous terrain was mostly suited to access by horseback. Not such a farfetched idea.

HARD TIMES

During the time my father was fighting across Italy and France, my mother, my little brother, and I were left in Morocco. This was a time of great hardship, as there was very little money and even less food. It wasn't that people couldn't afford the food, although that would probably have been the case; it was simply that there wasn't much food to be had because the Germans occupying France had cut off the food supply. We had been allowed to bring just 20 kilos of belongings with us out of Tunisia, so it was a case of making do with very little. We planted a vegetable garden even though the soil was dry but as soon as anything began to grow to the point where it was edible, people stole it in the night.

We were given ration tickets to be exchanged for a small amount of meat each month and to add to the misery the meat was mostly donkey or camel! If you have never eaten donkey or camel, take it from me you do not want to; it does not taste good. Any milk we could get was for my baby brother, Pierre, and was watered down so much that it could not have given him the nourishment he needed. After the war when we managed to get back to Brittany to visit my grandparents, my brother saw a square slab of something soft and yellow and asked what it was. "That is butter," my great aunt told him. He had never in all his seven years ever seen or tasted something that we all take for granted on a daily basis.

As a result, I used to go poaching and fishing to keep food on the table. The lack of food led me to develop a skill that I use to this very day—hunting with a slingshot. I took my slingshot everywhere and would shoot down everything I felt would help feed the family, sparrows, quail, dove; anything that flew, in fact. It was the only fresh meat we got to eat. My mother was angry and asked if I was taking my slingshot into school, but I was able to tell her no because on the way I hid it under the roots of an olive tree just outside the gate, then on my way home I would pick it up and go hunting for birds. It would take four or five small birds for each person, so I learned to be quite resourceful and persistent and was able to develop my skill at quite a distance, which helped as the birds would not let you get too close. While living in Morocco, we were able to get bread, Syrian style, and there were olives, oranges, and mandarins, but that was about the sum of it. There was no candy, no toys, in fact, nothing that could remotely be considered a luxury at all.

Horses Again

On May 2 of 1945, Soviet soldiers entered Berlin and took occupation of the city. Five days later, the Germans surrendered thus ending World War II in Europe. One month later, the Allied Supreme Command signed an agreement to divide Germany into four zones, each to be occupied by one of the Allies. The USSR occupied the eastern zone, Great Britain the northwestern zone, France the western zone, and the United States the southwestern zone. Berlin was in the Soviet zone and because it was the capitol it was agreed that it would be divided into four sectors with each of the victors having a part of the old capitol. In June, USSR leader Joseph Stalin established a communist-controlled government in Poland. Albania, Bulgaria, and Yugoslavia were also yielding to communism causing Winston Churchill to warn that "an Iron Curtain is being built across Europe" dividing communist from non-communist nations. By December, France, Britain and the United States had combined forces in their respective zones in Berlin. The communists took over the governments of Hungary, Romania, and Czechoslovakia and seemed unstoppable in their efforts to take over Eastern Europe.

It was during this time that my mother, Pierre, and I traveled to Germany to meet up with Father. General de Gaulle was president of France then (for the first time), and he did not like horses. This may have been due to his experiences at Saumur where I understand he had a hard time with his riding; nevertheless, he did not appreciate the mounted cavalry at all and had no interest in preserving the institution. He terminated the cavalry's active regiment ending the centuries-old tradition of the horse in combat. Just one squadron was sent back to France to be brought out on special occasions, mainly parades. An armored division of the cavalry continued, and there is an armored cavalry division at the French Cavalry School to this day, but the end of the war was difficult for my father who was left wondering what his future role would be.

Initially, Father was appointed a director of a prisoner-of-war camp where Polish soldiers, who had been forced to fight for Germany, were being held. He hated this work as he felt great compassion for the poor men and was helpless to do much except make life as easy as possible for them until they could eventually be returned to their homes and families.

During the German occupation, many of France's best stallions and broodmares had been taken by force and after the war French breeders were desperate to get their bloodlines back. Eventually, the French government asked my father to search for these horses; if they could be found the breeders could regenerate their Thoroughbred breeding program. This effort served to emphasize the value placed on the national racing and breeding industry. This project was near and dear to Father's heart and was so appealing that he willingly accepted the challenge. He managed to find some very well-bred horses including mares that were four and five years old, but who had never raced because of the war. Some of the breeding farms were so grateful to my father for finding these lost horses that they gave him some of these four- and five-year-olds that were too old to race as a thank you.

Father was delighted to resume his full-time career with horses when he was appointed Director of the French Equestrian Center in Berlin. The American, French, and British cavalry officers were denied the opportunity to take part in the sport that they loved while World War II raged and so as soon as conditions were right they went about organizing as many equestrian activities as possible in their spare time. Horse races as well as show-jumping and dressage competitions were hurriedly scheduled and kept the weekends pretty full. The British found a site at the old airport where they could hold races and my father eagerly joined in with that. The Americans mainly concentrated on show jumping with some combined tests added from time to time and Father organized races and horse shows as the French contribution to the activities. On weekends, each nation would take turns hosting the various competitions.

The French were based in the area of the old Polo Platz where Berliners had enjoyed playing polo before the war. The Polo Platz had belonged to Herr Geisler, whose son Harry had been trained at the Hanover Military School with classmate Willi Schulteis and many of the other dressage masters well respected for their knowledge of classical riding and their professionalism. Father kept his show jumpers, dressage horses, and racehorses at the Polo Platz and I was able to ride with him there, so life for me was once again worth living.

I had started riding a little at five or six years old and continued riding during the time we spent in Tunisia, but my serious riding began at 15 during the time we spent in Berlin. I learned about jumping and racing from father and about dressage from Herr Harry Geisler. My father was one of those people who could train a Grand Prix show-jumping horse, produce top-class racehorses and classically train a dressage horse to piaffe and passage—he was definitely at his best training horses. He was willing to teach me everything he knew about racing and jumping, but he was not comfortable teaching me dressage. At that time, it was politically impossible for my father to hire a German to be an instructor, so he hired Harry Geisler as a stable manager and told him that he had to teach me dressage. Harry provided very strict guidance and taught me to put my very first horse in passage at 16 years old. It is true I was the rider, but, and it is a strong but, I was merely the medium, the instrument, between Harry and the horse. I had no idea what I was doing and therefore was incapable of making the request of the horse myself, but to my complete amazement, the horse began to passage under me. Harry had a very long whip and walked along beside me teaching me how to apply the right aids to the horse to achieve my first high school movement.

The German cold blood horses were so hard to move forward, you had to kick and pull and ride with an immensely strong seat because they were so big and slow. The breed of horses back then dictated the type of "school" and the riding became synonymous with the school. The Germans preferred cold bloods and so the German School became equated with extremely strong riding. The French rode Anglo-Arabs, which were light and required more finesse and lightness of "feel."

Harry gave me my first serious and consistent teaching, so I learned more of the German school type of riding. It was to have a significant impact later when I went to Saumur and tried to ride the Anglo-Arabs the same way—such a disaster! The two years spent with Harry Geisler gave me a solid base regarding my position, seat, and use of the aids, all things that I was never to forget.

Meanwhile, the post-war political climate was deteriorating, and one of the first crises of the Cold War was gathering momentum. In March of 1948, the Soviets, wanting to extend their control, stopped Western trains bound for Berlin. The French, British, and Americans who occupied the other zones in the city actively opposed this Soviet takeover, which resulted in the Russians blockading Berlin. There was no fighting, but no one could get in or out as they attempted to get a stranglehold on the area. The Americans, British, and French, as well as the German people who lived in Berlin, were stuck. The Berlin Blockade effectively stopped all land, water, and rail access or egress. As it was impossible to get food, clothing, or medical supplies into the city, the American leaders organized what was called the Berlin Airlift, flying thousands of tons of supplies into Berlin's Tempelhof Airport. In fact, in just one day 7,000 tons of supplies were flown into the city: that amounted to a total of 895 flights within 24 hours, despite the fog, rain, and high winds. In this way, the Americans kept the city alive.

It was during this time that a tragedy hit our family, one from which we would never fully recover. My father had organized a steeplechase cross-country, a sport that is very popular in France even to this day. The word steeplechase comes from the practice that English farmers had of setting the distance for a race from one church steeple to another church steeple. Father's race began on the racetrack, followed a loop out into the country, carried on down a hill through some large trees, finally finishing back on the track. Father was a strategist and always worked out the fastest route. He knew exactly where he could save extra strides by cutting between the second-to-last tree and the last tree and so gain a few lengths advantage over the other jockeys.

On this day, I was riding in another race at the same meet and watched my father's race from the rail. I eagerly looked for him to be in the lead coming around the grandstand turn but he wasn't there. Something told me that things had gone horribly wrong. Down by the woods, people were milling around, and I could see the medics, but I did not expect it to be as bad as it was. My father's horse when faced with the path between the two trees had veered off in one direction when my father was leaning to steer him the other way. He had been thrown into one of the trees head first. It was merciful for him that he died a few hours later. He was the most active and self-motivated man I have ever known and may have continued to live in torment inside a brain so damaged that he would never have had an escape. He was only 41!

And so it was that my mother, my brother, and I were rendered almost destitute. We had no income. Our furniture and belongings in France had been destroyed and all we had left in the world was what we had been able to bring with us from North Africa—a mere 20 kilos each. And thanks to the blockade we were allowed to fly home from Berlin to the free zone with 20 kilos each once again. The anguish and pain in my mother's eyes are something I will never forget and this 17-year-old boy had to quickly grow up and take on the role of family head. The war years had done much to prepare me for that, but nothing could prepare me for the agony of losing my father.

2

A Horseman Is Born

From time to time in the course of one's life, people will cross your path that have a most profound impact in unexpected ways. You may only know them from a distance, but their words or their actions will leave an indelible impression, and you will be eternally grateful. One such person in my life was Colonel Frank Howley of the United States Army.

Colonel Howley was stationed in Berlin during the blockade and was, like many soldiers, involved in the equestrian endeavors at that time. He was very aware of the plight of my mother following the death of my father and knew that we were in difficult straits financially. This was true of many because no one escapes the ravages of war and the loss that it inflicts both in terms of human life and personal property, but Frank Howley took a personal interest in the Le Goff family, and I know that it was a mark of the respect he had for my father. He took it upon himself to organize a show-jumping competition as a fundraiser. It was held in the Berlin Olympic stadium famous for the 1936 Olympic Games and the money raised from that effort went a very, very long way towards my mother being able to buy a small house in Brittany and to take her family home. And so through the efforts and generosity of a man we did not know well the family had the means to begin to build a new life. I heard that Colonel Frank had retired in the South of France. I hope that his retirement was long, happy, and prosperous and he found peace in my old country in his later years.

THE EXERCISE BOY

Once back in Brittany, my mother became a school teacher and devoted herself to providing for her family. It was time for me to complete my education and I was enrolled in the local boarding school where I found math and physics boring and restrictive and could not wait to get outside to ride horses. The day I was to take my baccalaureate, an exam that French students have to pass to enter university, I made the grand decision that I had a better chance of winning a race than of passing my baccalaureate and so I went racing. I have to say I was right as I rode in a couple of races that day and won one! I would never recommend this course of action to any aspiring riders. I went back to school later and had to spend long hours in night school after a hard day's work in order to take classes that would eventually move the intelligence from my seat up to my brain where it should more properly reside—and it was a long and arduous climb! You will hear more about this later and learn additional techniques for achieving this goal, but as a horse-crazy teenager you would never have swayed me from my chosen path, and so it was that my working life began with sweeping floors and mucking out.

I set out from home confident that I would be able to find a job with racehorses and fulfill my passion for the racing game. I packed my little suitcase with three pairs of socks, three sets of underwear, and three shirts and set off for Paris. I had no idea where I would sleep but with all the optimism of youth, I figured something would turn up and my ideal job would be waiting for me.

Someone was looking down on me. I happened to stop by the yard of Willy Head, patriarch of the Head dynasty of jockeys and trainers. Willy was an ex-steeplechase jockey who had turned trainer and moved to Maison Lafitte, the famous Thoroughbred training center outside of Paris. His sons Peter and Alec were also trainers and Alec's daughter Cricket is still a famous trainer in Europe. Willy's grandson, Freddie Head was a leading jockey on the flat for many years. Willy Head gave me my first job as a stable lad. This auspicious moment was the birth of Jack Le Goff the horseman and my introduction to hard but rewarding work. Never before had I been the one to do the chores in the stable because as the son of the Director of Equestrian Programs for the Army in Berlin my horses had been brought out groomed and saddled up ready for me to mount. Now I had hands-on training in the care and keeping of the horses and I loved it. Now the learning days started in earnest.

I managed to find lodging with a family about 10 miles away from the stables. The gates to the yard opened at six in the morning sharp. If you were not there, they closed again, and you were out of luck. I had to bicycle there in rain, wind, and snow, up the hill and down the hill (the downhill part was the best) however it meant I was riding to work in the dark and home again in the dark. I still can't remember much about the scenery! Fortunately, it wasn't long before Willy needed someone to ride and they put me up on a horse, which made all the hard work fade away, and I started riding for him as an exercise boy.

About six months after this, I went home to see my mother and brother in Brittany. Mother had managed to enroll Pierre in a very fancy military boarding school, and it appeared he was bound for a military career. Naturally, I couldn't keep away from horses for very long and during my visit, I went to see a local trainer who lived about five miles away. He had some flat race and steeplechase horses in his barn and when he found out I could ride he asked me to gallop a couple of horses while I was there. Immediately he offered me a job, and that is how I made the transition from stable lad to stable jockey. I took out a gentleman's license to race and did not return to Maison Lafitte, which I think pleased mother greatly. I was still riding the bike early in the morning to get to the stables, but galloping the racehorses on the beach every day more than made it worthwhile. In fact, there were a couple of race meets held on the beach at that time, and I was able to ride in those.

15 POUNDS

At nineteen and 6 feet 2 inches, it was only going to be a matter of time before weight problems brought an end to my race riding. I was able to ride at 128 to 130 pounds for a while on the flat; over fences I could go to 132 pounds, but it was always a battle, and my weight fluctuated up and down. After one flat race, I was so weak from dieting that I fainted in the jockey's room and thought it was time I found another career.

While exploring my options for a career in the horse world, the one that came out on top of my list was the Cadre Noir in Saumur. However, the only way to gain entrance to the Cadre Noir at that time was through the Army and at the rank of *Marechal des Logis* no less. I made my application to the Army while I was riding in races and at my physical, the doctor after checking me over said, "Young man, I cannot pass you for entry into the army. You are 6 foot 2 inches and you weigh 127 pounds. There must be something wrong with you." I replied, "Doctor, I am a jockey riding in steeplechases, and if you give me three weeks I promise you I can put on 15 pounds." And how I enjoyed the next few weeks, returning, eventually, to the doctor's office carrying a little more than the minimum amount. As a result, I was given the go-ahead to enlist as a private.

I had to go through basic training and took the corporal course followed by the *Marechal des Logis* course for non-commissioned officers. I graduated from that first in my class and then finally having achieved the rank of *Marechal des Logis*, I had access to the entrance exam, which would allow me into the course to become a member of the Cadre Noir. I passed this pretty easily thanks to my background in dressage, racing, and show jumping and entered the nine-month course, which I had heard was extremely hard. That didn't even come close to telling the real story!

The students rode eight horses a day for a total of eight hours or more. For the first three months, six of those eight hours were without stirrups, so the breeches were more often red with blood than any other color. It was brutal, and within days the flesh on my legs and derriere was red raw and bleeding. Scabs would form and the hardest days were when the scabs would be worn off. We had to wash our breeches every day—not such a simple matter of throwing them in the washer and popping them in the dryer as it is today. We had to have a few pairs to allow for drying time!

In the evening, we had to do book work, and we all spent that time sitting in buckets of water with a chemical in it to toughen the skin. As time progressed and you were hardy enough to stick with the program, it started to become less painful until eventually, it didn't affect you anymore. It all sounds quite barbaric today, but the exercise was designed to find those tough enough to stick with it. Many wanted to join the Cadre Noir and there were never enough places so only the best and the toughest survived. I must have had skin like a rhinoceros because I was a survivor of the course.

I graduated head of my class, which qualified me for the privilege of becoming an under-riding master—an offer that I accepted without need for further consideration. Soon after, I was given the black uniform of the Cadre Noir and put it on. I looked in the mirror and was very impressed with myself. "I am an under-riding master in the Cadre Noir at Saumur, and it doesn't come much better than that," thought I. In my defense, I was probably, up to that time at least, the youngest under-riding master ever, and I figured I was pretty big stuff. I was misguided enough to believe that the knowledge and the science came with the uniform. Very quickly, the Cadre Noir disabused me of that notion and brought me down to a quite painful reality. Disenchantment with myself and my misconceptions came quickly and most thoroughly. Without my knowing it, the older riding masters were observing me and were eager and willing to participate in my disillusionment. Deflating the ego was an art well practiced and perfected by my superiors and elders.

THE BEAUTY OF LIGHTNESS

Shortly after becoming a member of the Cadre Noir, I married the daughter of a prominent Saumur family, Pauline Kralicek. We met at a town dance that she attended with a chaperone. Pauline was the daughter of Czechoslovakian Count Kralicek. We soon had two children, Martine and Dominique, and several years later had a third child, Cyrille.

Meanwhile, I was lucky enough to catch the eye of Colonel Margot the chief *ecuyer*, the head riding master who in my book is the best, most elegant, most accomplished dressage rider I ever met in my life. He was a phenomenon and the ultimate horseman in my mind: the one I most wanted to emulate. He could get on any ordinary horse and make him look like a top flight horse. I was Colonel Margot's protégé, and his "victim" and God knows it was not an easy position. He was a very, very tough guy and couldn't understand why we could not ride as he did, but I considered it a great honor and privilege to work under him. It was an extremely testing time for me as it was not unusual for the colonel to call me names. *"Vous etes mauvais,"* he would yell. *"Vous etes un imbécile."* I knew though that he didn't really mean that. In fact, he was a very shy person and hid behind his arrogant behavior. I got to know him very well over the years and had a tremendous respect and admiration for him.

We would start work very early in the morning and try to have everything completed and shipshape for 5:00 p.m. At this time, he would send his groom to fetch me as he had me ride many of his horses and warm them up for him. No one was allowed to ride in the arena at this time except me because I was riding Colonel Margot's horses.

He was so brilliant in the saddle that he had a difficult time understanding why an ordinary person could not feel and ride like he did. Being so brilliant doesn't always help people be the best teachers. He would tell me to go into an extended trot, and then he would shout at me in French, "Come here! Get off that horse! You do not understand anything." He was just trying to get the best out of me and make me angry enough to work harder, and it worked very well. He would tell me to get off, and he would get on and ride the horse. I would watch him intently and try to see what he was doing so that I could learn his way as he could not always find the words to describe the finer nuances of what he wanted me to achieve.

It was Colonel Margot who taught me the beauty of lightness. He watched me kicking and pulling and grinding with my seat on one of these beautifully light, elegant Anglo-Arabs. "What are you doing?" he screamed. "You are not riding one of those German cold-bloods now. Get off and watch!" There were other things that he said to me but I hope that many young riders will read this book and the publishers would not allow those words to be printed! Today the German horses have been infused with Thoroughbred blood, and there is a lot more quality to them than back in the forties and fifties.

In 1956, I was part of the Cadre Noir team that was asked to perform a demonstration ride at the Olympic Games in Stockholm. Being somewhat obsessive about all things equestrian I used the free time to watch the Olympic show jumping. In the warm-up area, it was an education in itself just watching the German rider Fritz Thiedemann, who was a diminutive man, riding a typical big, elephant-size German horse called Meteor. He had an exceedingly long dressage whip, which was constantly in use—zap zapping, rein back, kick, kick, zap, zap, not abusively but enough to get the attention. At first, the horse didn't take any notice whatsoever and he dropped rails on every warm-up fence, but after 20 minutes, the horse was breathing steam down his nostrils and out of his ears. That's what it took to get the horse going. He went into the ring, his eyes were popping out of his head, but he jumped a clear round. Meteor helped Germany to win the team gold medal that year and placed fourth individually. In his career, he won the individual bronze in Helsinki, placed second in the 1956 World Championships and won a second team gold medal in Rome. None of that would have happened without Fritz lighting the fire under him.

THE STOCKHOLM OLYMPICS

At that time, I was actively competing in eventing while at the Cadre Noir, so naturally I had a keen interest in the cross-country course at Stockholm and spent some time walking it and analyzing the fences. The Stockholm Olympics were a bit of an anomaly as the '56 Olympics were held in Australia. Due to the stringent quarantine regulations Downunder, the equestrian events had to be held elsewhere, and Stockholm was chosen as the venue. While the atmosphere was very "horsey" it was different and lacked that special "Olympic" feel that comes from having athletes from all sports and all countries in one place at the same time. The opening ceremonies go a long way to firing everyone up and so Stockholm '56 was a bit of an anti-climax.

Things were very different back then. The Russian team had only one helmet for three riders, and they had to keep passing it from one to the other after each performance.

The cross-country course was not easy by any means, and it was very basic regarding materials and construction, and I would have to say it was unsafe. Ditches at that time were not revetted as they are today. The footing became very slippery, and the horses just could not find the traction to take off and ended falling in the ditch. America's Jack Burton (Major General Jonathan R. Burton) was one of the numerous victims of this fence, but he got back on and even with a concussion managed to complete the course, including that awful and unnecessary run-in on Phase E.

I felt it was almost as though riders were sent out on this course as if for battle. "Go forward young man, it is for your country." The appellation of the sport then was "The Military." No kidding!

Nevertheless, my determination to compete in an Olympic Games increased, and it was back to Saumur I went with every intention of making the French team in 1960. Later in 1956, I won the French Eventing Championship, and was the leading rider in eventing on a number of occasions throughout those years leading up to Rome. I would have liked to have competed seriously in show jumping but without a sponsor, it was impossible to acquire the number of horses necessary to allow me to be competitive. In show jumping you need to have multiple horses to ride and constantly be jumping fences in order to become practiced enough to be success-ful—you also have to be devoted to it, and eventing always had my heart. As the youngest riding master I was given whatever horses were left over after the senior riding masters had taken their pick and since I was not born with the wealth I deserved, I concentrated on eventing.

3

MAKING THE TEAM!

Thanks to Colonel Margot, I was picked to represent France on the Three-day Event Team in the 1960 Olympic Games in Rome. Without him, it surely would not have happened. There were a number of trials throughout France in that last year leading to the Games, and I was fortunate enough to be leading rider throughout that period. One would have thought I was a dead certainty for the team, and I would have been today except that team selection for the Olympics at that time was in the hands of the military "head honchos." In the Cadre Noir, which was still run by the Army, I was a riding master, but in the regular army, I was a non-commissioned officer. This fact and the fact that I was in a black uniform did not go very well with the powers that be in the Army. I had two strikes against me, and I cannot imagine that Colonel Fresson, who was in charge of the Army teams at the Fontainebleau Training Center, was happy as he must have wanted his own three-day riders on the team. Thank God the chef d'equipe was Colonel Margot. He didn't care. He wanted me on the team because he said I was the best rider France had at the time.

A Distinct Advantage

If my recollection does not fail me, the endurance day in Rome was the longest of the post-World War II era. The steeplechase was 4,500 meters, cross-country was 8,100 meters, add to this the infamous 2,000 meters of Phase E and you are looking at some tired horses. The roads and tracks only added to the extreme endurance factor as they were very long and very dusty.

The order in which each team will go is chosen randomly; today it is done by a computer, but back then it was by drawing from a hat. One hat was used to draw the number of go, and another hat was used to draw the country for that order of go. The first rider on each team competes and when all the teams have sent out their first rider then the second rider on each team competes, and so it proceeds until all of the riders on all of the teams have competed. In the drawing, Team France drew the number right behind Team Australia. On Endurance day, I was out on Roads and Tracks and saw an Australian rider coming toward me. I couldn't believe it. I knew I was on the right track and had not missed a flag, so this Aussie must be off course! I kept on going.

My teammates had the same experience, and we were all wondering what the Australians were doing. We found out. They had concluded that they could cut out a huge section of this phase as there were no compulsory flags at the far end of the roads and tracks. The free-spirited Australians used their ingenuity and found a better way, but those of us with a strict military tradition of discipline and of following rules to the letter did not use the same creative thinking and were covering all those extra kilometers, which were in fact technically unnecessary! This gave them and their horses a distinct advantage as the added distance took a tremendous toll on all the other horses, including ours. The army discipline did not work for us there!

The Rome Olympics were a turning point in the development of the sport and the way of competing. Why? Because the Australians proved that you could be way down the order after dressage and yet with very fast horses who were brilliant jumpers on the cross-country (and they were the best there was by a long shot at the time) riders could pull up to the top of the scoreboard if they could get within the time required.

The Australians certainly made me as a rider and trainer rethink my whole program. When I came through the finish line of that darn Phase E (2,000 meters of flat galloping after the cross-country) I didn't have to pull up, I simply had to stop riding my mare and she dropped to a walk immediately because she was so pooped. I turned around to weigh in and saw the Australian right after me cantering through the finish as fresh as if he were just starting. I asked the steward, "Where is he coming from?" "From the same place you came from," was the answer. This could not be possible; comparing my horse to the Australian's was like night and day. There was something wrong here.

I thought about the breeding. My mare Image was a mutt, sired by a trotter out of an Anglo-Arab mare. Her conformation was less than ideal, and her gaits were influenced by her sire (trotters in France do not pace as they do in the States and they do not have the most fluid movement), and she would never have won a dressage class. She would not have been a candidate for steeplechasing as she was not fast enough and her limited jumping ability would not have made her sought after by the show jumpers. What she did have was an immense heart, and she had great intelligence. She was generous and smart and never had a fall in her entire career because she had that fifth leg everywhere and, as far as I can remember, she never had a stop or run out on any cross-country course. She had done an amazing job and jumped clean, but she was completely done. Either we had the wrong horses or we were not training them properly. The Australians forced me to look at the type of horses needed, but most of all their preparation intrigued me. What had they done and how had they done it?

The course in Rome was big, and there was no doubt that the Australians had created a new trend regarding competition preparation for both horses and riders. They had to get Bill Roycroft back in the saddle to show jump as one of the other team horses could not compete on the final day. Bill had been taken to the hospital with a broken collarbone after his cross-country round, but without his score, they would not be able to complete a team. Bill was brilliant as well as tough and, riding with the reins in only one hand, he jumped a clear round under those adverse conditions. Today, the competition's medical officer would not have allowed him to ride, but no such rules were in place then, and the Australians won the team gold medal that day thanks to Bill. His teammates, Laurence Robert Morgan and Neale John Lavis, won the gold and silver on Salad Days and Mirrabooka respectively. Anton S. Buhler of Switzerland won the bronze and Image and I were sixth individually. The French team of Capt. Guy Lefrant, Jehan le Roy, Pierre Durand, and I won the bronze medal behind the Swiss who won the silver.

The difficulty of Rome's cross-country course was highlighted by the fact that 73 riders started and only 35 completed—less than 50 percent! Out of 18 teams, only six finished. I doubt that course would pass the inspection of any Course Advisor, Technical Delegate or Ground Jury today, but that was the way of courses all those years ago. While some of the ditches had some revetting, an improvement over Stockholm, it was not strong enough and gave way. The poles used on the fences were still thin, and no changes had been made to the uprightness of the verticals. Furthermore, I had never seen a jump anything like "the drainpipe." This fence came toward the end of the course and was made up of sections of huge concrete drainpipes set side by side so that when you approached the jump you could see right through the pipes. The designer had then put a very thin rail across the top of the pipes. I am tall and when I was walking the course, it began to rain. I sat in this pipe quite comfortably when sheltering from the rain, which gives you an idea of the size. Adding to the difficulty was the way the land fell away on the landing side. The whole fence required a supremely bold and forward horse.

MY TURN

As I have mentioned, there were some inter-regimental politics going on with the French team prior to my being selected. All of this might explain why, after a pretty good cross-country round in Rome and before the show jumping, Colonel Fresson informed me that I was on the list to go to fight in Algeria. Not a good thing to do when you are trying to focus on finishing the Games with a clear round to keep the team in a medal position. I smiled and said it was fine with me, but I didn't think it was a particularly elegant thing to do, and there is no doubt that it could have waited until after the show jumping was over.

General Noiret held the highest ranking in the brass of the French Army. He had been in the Cadre Noir in his younger days and, having an interest in all the equestrian sports, had come to Rome to watch the Olympics as a spectator. He was my father's commanding officer and had been in Berlin on that fateful date, April 25, 1948. General Noiret heard that I was on the list to go to Algeria, and he had been told of the manner in which I had been notified. He was not impressed and sought me out. He said, "I can find a lot of lieutenants to command a platoon, but I don't have too many riders that can represent France in international competition like you. So if you don't want to go to Algeria just say so." I looked at him with the greatest respect and admiration and said, "Sir, it is my turn; I want to go because if I don't go someone else will have to go in my place." General Noiret looked at me with a smile and said, "You are as stubborn as your father, aren't you?" It was a compliment I was proud to accept.

This episode gives an interesting insight into the protocol in place not only with the military but also within the International Olympic

Committee's thinking in the 1950s. In 1956, there had been a sig-nificant development at the Stockholm Olympics. Sergeant Petrus Kastenman, who won the individual gold medal on Illuster, was a non-commissioned officer in the Swedish cavalry school. Kasten-man had proved himself a leading light in eventing, but he was of a lower rank (that of Master Sergeant) and the Olympic rules at that time allowed for participation by "officers and (civilian) gentlemen" only, excluding any other rank of the Army, and women of course. A Master-Sergeant just wouldn't do. So Sweden promoted Kastenman to a higher rank of officer two or three months before the Olym-pics. In reality, Kastenman was made officer just for the occasion of the Stockholm games. He won the gold and then quite soon after-ward the Swedish military downgraded him to his previous rank of a non-commissioned officer. It was the most stupid thing they could have done, and they got caught. The International Olympic Committee (IOC) said if Sweden insisted on downgrading him they would take the gold medal away. Sweden, of course, did not want to let that happen so reinstated him. Later, the Olympic rule was changed to allow non-commissioned officers to compete, but it was thanks to Kastenman setting this precedent that I was able to ride in the Olympics in 1960.

My greatest debt though was to Colonel Margot without whom I would never have been on that Olympic team. I will always cherish and remember with great humility and pride the years I spent with the maestro and mentor. His willingness to put himself out and stand up against his colleagues and superiors in the army because of his belief in me and my abilities was inspiring and motivated me to work harder at everything I did. I owe him much. Saddened as I was to say goodbye to this period of my life, I had a duty to perform in Algeria.

4

AND OFF TO WAR I WENT

After many years of French colonial rule, the peoples of Vietnam, Cambodia, and Laos wanted their independence. The unrest and rebellion escalated into the Vietnam War. Communism was on the rise, and the people of Indo-China were under a lot of pressure from the Communists to capitulate. Following the battle of Dien Bien Phu and the signing of the Evian Accord, which gave Indo-China its independence from France, the French withdrew and the United States, attempting to control the spread of communism, moved in soon after.

Algeria was a French state, and the Algerian men did their military service as soldiers of the French Army under the same terms and conditions as all young Frenchmen. Algerians served in the French Army in World Wars I and II and Vietnam. Soon after the French pulled out of Vietnam, some Algerians felt that Algeria, like Indo-China, should also be independent of France and within a short time a rebellion began. The rebel forces were very experienced and well-organized fighters as some had received military training in France and had also served one, and in some cases even two, terms in the French army in Vietnam. In an attempt to put down the Algerian rebellion and keep Algeria under French rule, General de Gaulle returned to power.

This then was the war that I went to fight following the Rome Olympics. Having lived so long in North Africa as a youngster, I spoke Arabic fluently, which made me a prime candidate as an intelligence officer. My little brother Pierre, now a career officer in the French Army having attended St. Cyr, the French equivalent of West Point, was also posted to Algeria and from time to time our paths would cross.

THE CAVALRY

The military powers realized that they had an almost impossible job controlling the situation with the rebel forces in the Atlas Mountains of Algeria. The hostile and inhospitable nature of the terrain prohibited the use of modern military equipment. The army decided that the best way to control the high plateau and the mountains was to bring back horse regiments, which would be more mobile than armored trucks and able to get into places those vehicles could not access. The army had a problem: they had no staff that knew anything about horses anymore. So they drafted back people from Saumur and any other soldiers who had ever been involved with horses in sport and proceeded to resurrect three mounted Spahis Regiments.

The greatest irony was that my father was in the last mounted cavalry regiment from Morocco in World War II, and in 1960, just a few years later, I was called back in the regular army to serve in the 23rd Mounted Regiment of Algerian Spahis. This regiment was made up of 90 percent native Algerians who were now fighting against their fellow countrymen.

Life became about as different as it was possible to get. For two years the only bath we could get was a sand bath. There is practically no water in that region and whatever water there is available is very precious and kept solely for drinking. Occasionally airplanes would drop containers of water when things got desperate, but this was dangerous as it would indicate to the enemy where we were. So we did what the desert people do and bathed in the sand. We would strip off our clothes and put on a *djellaba*, a large roomy garment that afforded some privacy. The best are made of camel hairs which protect from heat and cold and which are used by the Tuareg and other nomadic tribes. Under cover of the *djellaba*, we would take handfuls of fine sand and rub it all over our skin. You would be amazed at how effective this is. The exfoliating properties of the sand remove all traces of dirt, sweat, and odor and leave your skin feeling fresh and smooth and strangest of all you smell pretty good too. I was unable to shave at all and this, combined with a suntan, meant I could easily have passed for a native Algerian. I also developed the fine art of peeing from the back of my horse—a dismounted soldier is an easy target for the enemy!

It was a terrible war and one that split Algerian families down the middle. Some young Algerian men were fighting for the French against their brothers who had joined the rebellion. The rebels were fighting for freedom and autonomy and as some of the French-Algerian soldiers began to fully understand the evolution of the war they would switch sides. My valet had a brother in the Algerian rebel army and one night he disappeared to join his brother. Usually, when these men left like this, they would kill the French military in their company, usually their senior officer, to prove their loyalty to the Algerian cause. Thankfully, my valet just left!

Some soldiers who were not in the regular French army were called Harkis. These were units of all native Algerian combat soldiers, some of whom came from the rebel side, and who thought that with de Gaulle coming back to power they should ally themselves with the French. When the tide began to turn, they couldn't go back and switch sides again for fear of being killed by the rebels. I was finally sent back to France with the mission to pick up different groups of Harkis and their families from the south of Algeria and take them back to

France. I took 800 of them to Oran Harbor for the journey across the Mediterranean back to France. They were eventually placed in camps, and it took the authorities a long time to integrate them into French society. In fact, they never were completely integrated; rather, they were diluted into the existing Algerian community and were indistinguishable from the Algerians only interested in making money. These people risked not only their lives for France but also became pariahs in their homeland. They were in effect "between countries" and it was heartbreaking to see them treated so carelessly.

INTERVAL TRAINING

Once back in France, I did not return to Saumur but was stationed at the Fontainebleau Training Center where I resumed my passion for eventing. At the end of 1962, the Ministry of Sport held a meeting for all the coaches of all the sports where they discussed the new and different techniques in coaching, training, sports psychology, and other developments. A fascinating lecture was given by a trainer in Track and Field on something called "interval training." This lecture triggered my thinking, and I remembered the Australians at the Rome Olympics and my promise to myself to research conditioning techniques. A well-known trainer of Standardbred racehorses had been experimenting with interval training with great success, and this aroused my interest even more. I began an in-depth study of interval training and how it could work for event horses. I put one-third of the horses in my care into this program to see how their fitness level would compare to the horses conditioned using my former program. It became very obvious that these horses got very fit very quickly, so much so that it became a problem—they were almost unmanageable in dressage because they did not know how to cope with their new level of fitness. After this, I began to experiment by using interval training in conjunction with some of the principles I used when conditioning and training racehorses years before. Eventually, I came up with a refined system that proved to be very efficient in getting the horses fit, sound, and sane to compete at the highest levels.

One of the reasons I elected to go to Fontainebleau and not return to the Cadre Noir in Saumur was the breakdown of my marriage. The marriage had not been totally successful, and it had certainly not been helped by my two years away at war. During my second year away, the relationship broke down irretrievably. So with the marriage over, I buried myself in my riding and worked toward a place on the team at the Tokyo Olympics in 1964, but during every free weekend, I drove back to Saumur to spend time with my three children.

5

WOMEN AND A CHANGING SPORT

The face of the Olympic Three-day Event was changing and never more so than in Tokyo in 1964 when the first woman rider was allowed to compete. As mentioned before, Olympic competition was limited up until this time to officers and civilian gentlemen. It had been thought that women would not be able to withstand the rigors of such a competition. The selection of Lana DuPont (now Wright) and Mr. Wister for the US team put an end to all that and opened the door for women from all nations to put the Olympics on their agendas. God knows since then women have proven that they are more than capable of competing side by side with men, often standing above them on the Olympic podium. Lana clearly demonstrated that women are every bit as tough as men when it comes to riding cross-country. It had always been feared that if a woman fell it was very unlikely that she would get back on and finish for the team. Lana proved that this was a fallacy as she did just that and kept the US team in contention.

There were many countries that were adamant that women would never ride on their teams and even today there are a few that still feel that way, but they are not vocal about it. One of the greatest event riders of all time, Britain's Sheila Wilcox, was prevented from ever competing in an Olympic Games. Sheila won Badminton three times, and in 1957 at the age of 21 became the European Champion in Copenhagen, but she was never allowed to reach the ultimate goal of the Olympic Games because she was a woman. Lana DuPont Wright opened the Olympic door and today women are often fiercer competitors than many of the men. They certainly dominate the standings frequently and have proven beyond a doubt that all those old prejudices had no real foundation.

It is thanks to Lana and other women equestrian pioneers who refused to let tradition hinder the progress and development of the Olympic movement that we have a much more open and equitable sport without the archaic restrictions of class and gender. And, I might add, one made more attractive to the media because men and women do compete against each other on equal terms.

Tokyo 1964

Tokyo gave a good perspective of Olympic three-day competition in general but in particular underlined the influence of the cross-country, and I had a good opportunity to develop a feel for how courses were evolving. The steeplechase was classic, but I remember an incident on roads and tracks particularly where one stretch ran along a paved street. The sidewalks were dirt as opposed to the tarmac on the road, so I tried to ride on the sidewalk to save my horse's legs. Soon my way was barred by a Japanese soldier with a gun who signaled to me in no uncertain way that I was to go on the road. I obeyed but guess what, 100 yards farther on I was back on the sidewalk. Let this unsympathetic, non-equestrian soldier put that in his pipe and smoke it!

The cross-country course had a good diversity of obstacles, but again it was considerably easier than Rome. The course was not as big, and I felt it was quite a step down regarding the size and difficulty of the cross-country fences. The combination fences had lines that required more accurate riding, a sign that the technicality was increasing. The fences were fairly well built for that era, but it was still old-fashioned regarding the materials used.

My horse Leopard and I were named to the French Team for Tokyo where we placed twenty-third, and the team finished in eighth place overall.

The French Equestrian Team was going through a very difficult time. Up to that point, the Army had been in control of the international equestrian teams, but civilian riders were starting to challenge the army's control. Our three-day event team in Tokyo had a very hard time as the different levels of responsibility created disorganization and confusion. In fact, no one was in charge, and a team without a coach is bound to be unsuccessful.

With two Olympic Games behind me and my Army career-ending, it was time to consider my future options. Planning for a new and different life began in earnest.

PART II

THE COACHING YEARS

"It is helpful for me to have a French accent. One can charge more for dressage lessons."

6

THE BEST LAID PLANS

The Tokyo Olympics over, I returned to France and contemplated my future. I had served more than 15 years in the Army and in a few short months would be eligible for a lifetime pension. I began to make plans to set up a private business teaching and training while at the same time continuing with my competitive riding. I was once again the leading rider in France, enjoying some very good wins at events and felt that this would be the ideal time to strike out on my own. The decision made, I began reorganizing my professional life.

A phone call from the French Federation turned my plan on its head. Would I be interested in becoming the coach of the French Three-Day Event Team? This surprised me as up to that point the Army had been in charge of all the teams in equestrian disciplines, and now that I was a civilian I did not think I would be considered. Things were changing, even in the Army. It had always been a dream of mine to coach an international team, and here I was being given that chance straight off the bat. The decision was a tough one though as the Federation made it clear that if I accepted the position, I would have to stop competing. I was 36 years old and felt I had a good few years of top-level competition in me, but since I was not a man of independent means I had to be practical and it was tempting to think about the financial security this offer would provide. I knew my years at Saumur would stand me in good stead, as would my experience on two Olympic teams. I was no stranger to the pressures facing the riders, and I knew how vital the role of coach is in converting those pressures and stress into positives and making them work for the success of the team. So I said yes and in April 1965, I began a career as an Olympic coach that would last for close to 30 years.

I had just begun coaching the French senior team when I got another call from the Federation asking me if I would be willing to help three riders from Japan. The Japanese Federation wanted their riders to gain experience in Europe and had asked if the French would be willing to assist them. Naturally, I said yes and Dr. Mikio Chiba, Minpei Shirai and Masao Ogawa arrived at Fontainebleau and stayed with me until after the 1968 Olympic Games in Mexico.

A Fall and a Rise

During this time, tragedy decided that it had not finished with the Le Goff family. I was vacationing with my two older children on an island off the coast of Brittany when I saw two gendarmes approaching. Right away, it gave me the chills. I knew something was wrong. They handed me a telegram. Pierre, my brother and best friend, died in a car accident coming back from a three-day event in Haras du Pin. He left a beautiful wife and two children. When Father died, I accepted his death because it was an accident. When Pierre died, I questioned God because it was so unfair. He was a brilliant man, a wonderful guy with a great future ahead of him. Why had God taken him, a person who had done no wrong, instead of me, the "rogue" of the family?

This tragedy was more than I could take. The excruciating agony of that loss lingered a long, long time and, along with the loss of my marriage, caused me to lose my faith. It was then that I decided, right or wrong if life is so short then live it to the fullest extent possible.

I began to lead a very social existence. For the next year or so I enjoyed life to the fullest possible. I partied, I had many girlfriends, and I kept winning every competition. It was as if I could not lose. I stretched myself to the limit, having just a wonderful time. I often stayed up late. I drank a lot, too much, and enjoyed having many female admirers, some of whom were married and looking for fun. I was perfectly happy to comply with their wishes. Then, one day, I took several horses to a horse show. I rode in several classes during the show and never got into the ribbons. And the big bell rang when my groom came to me and said, "Sir, this has got to stop, or things are going to continue in this direction." It was a very good wake-up call.

During this time, I met a young woman, Marie-Madeleine Giraud, who became my great friend. Madeleine worked for NATO, and we met in the NATO mess hall. We often had meals together at the same table, and Madeleine was aware of my troubled love life.

We realized that the friendship might develop into something more, but Madeleine was leaving for Hong Kong where she had already accepted a job, before our closer acquaintance. So we agreed that when she returned if we felt the same way about each other, we would solidify our union.

And so it was that I married for the second time in my life in June 1966. Madeleine and I settled in Fontainebleau where I continued preparing the team for the 1968 Olympics and where Madeleine gave birth to our two children, Florence and Corinne, who along with Martine, Dominique, and Cyrille have been the greatest pleasures and the greatest achievements of my life.

Meanwhile, I was on the lookout for up-and-coming talent to train for future teams and had been casting my eye around for junior riders to prepare for the future. It was a good thing I had! I hadn't even finished setting up a junior program when in 1967 I got a call from Lt. Col. R.B. (Babe) Moseley, who was a driving force behind British eventing and who had a specific interest in the British juniors and young riders, seeing them as the foundation of future international teams.

"Jack," he said. "I want to organize a Junior European Championships. Will you bring a team if I can put it together?"

"Yes Sir!" said I. "When are you thinking of doing this?"

"You have about three weeks," said Colonel Moseley. He did tell me afterward that he thought I would be the only one crazy enough to give it a shot!

Now I had my work cut out for me and had to set about finding some juniors to make a team. I mustered three riders, one of whom had his own horse and two others whom I mounted on Army horses that were under my care. I asked the French Federation for some financial assistance, but while they were interested in the project, there was no money to help fund the trip. To keep costs down, I drove the horse van and acted as the agent for the team during the shipping across the Channel to and from England. That was a miserable job. There was so much paperwork and bureaucracy, and you don't know what to expect until you have to do it. I vowed never again! Still, we got the juniors to Eridge in England and to the first Junior European Championships ever held.

There were two teams, France and Britain. Britain had 12 riders and we had three. French rider Alain Souchon and Roi d'Asturie won the gold medal, Philippe Giraud, and Saphir d'Eau the bronze, and P. Santoni and Loufoque were fourth, which put the team in the lead overall. The second placed rider was Britain's Richard Walker with Pasha. The next year this pair won gold and went on the following year to win Badminton, making Richard the youngest rider to win

THE ROLES WE PLAY

THE ROLE OF THE TRAINER

Trainers as the name implies train the horses and teach the riders at home on a regular basis. They teach the rider how to ride and improve his or her skills while at the same time schooling the horses in the various phases with the goal of preparing them both for competition.

I was once asked by a journalist to explain what a trainer does. My profound and philosophical response was that the trainer makes the rider do what he doesn't want to do on his own!

THE ROLE OF THE COACH

The coach is the person at the competition charged with producing the very best performance possible from horse and rider. The coach capitalizes on the training the horse and rider have received up to this point. Obviously, this includes warming the horse and rider up before entering the arena, walking courses, and devising the tactics and technical approach for each phase of the competition. This often means making sure that the riders are totally aware of the rules that include knowing what to do when things are not going according to Plan A. For example, if a rider has had a disobedience on the cross-country course, particularly in a combination, he has to know exactly what to do to avoid more penalties, which necessitates a good knowledge of the rules and their interpretation.

THE ROLE OF THE CHEF D'EQUIPE

The chef d'equipe liaises between the organizing committee, the Ground Jury and the team at all the major international competitions. He attends all the meetings and the draw, and communicates all of

the information concerning the running of the competition to the rid-
ers. This includes the training schedule of where and when horses
can gallop and school; where vehicles are allowed to go or not go
and at what times; and any changes that may have to be made to the
cross-country course. The chef d'equipe is usually responsible for the
order of go in the team.

The Role of the Chef de Mission

The chef de mission comes into play at championships where several
disciplines are involved such as the Olympic Games and the World
Equestrian Games. The three equestrian Olympic disciplines have been
and still are dressage, show jumping, and eventing. At the World Eques-
trian Games, in addition to the three Olympic disciplines, there are
vaulting, driving, endurance, and reining. The chef de mission commu-
nicates between the organizing committee and each team discipline.
He is the top authority for coordination and administration and has no
responsibility for coaching any of the teams.

In the United States, the trainer, coach, and chef d'equipe can be the
same person as was true in my case and with Bert de Némethy who so

the world's greatest three-day event, surely proof that a solid junior
program helps to produce tomorrow's stars.

The French won the gold medal, which I didn't think was bad considering they had only been together in training for about three
weeks. This win gave France the privilege of hosting the following
year's championships, which we held at the Craon racetrack. That
second year 11 nations were represented, and the Junior European

ably coached the USET Show Jumping Team. While this system creates a great deal of work in many ways, it is easier to operate because you have such an in-depth knowledge of the team riders and horses.

As Director of the Team Three-Day Training Center, I was also responsible for making all the arrangements necessary to take the team abroad and for ensuring that not only was the team successful in competition but also that the entire operation ran smoothly. I had to make reservations for planes and hotels; secure stabling for the horses before shipping to the competition; hire horse vans; make the entries and numerous other clerical jobs that are part of international competition. In those days, the team was limited in funds and every dollar raised went to support the competitive effort. I was also responsible for keeping the books. The day often started before 7:00 a.m. and ended after 10 at night. Bookkeeping was the last thing to do each day and had to be done because when you got back to headquarters, you were expected to be able to account for every payment and every receipt. In short, when away from home I was trainer, coach, accountant, travel agent, and Captain of the Love Boat.

Championships were well and truly underway thanks to the vision and hard work of Colonel Babe Moseley.

Punchestown European Championships 1967

Attention was now on the senior team as they prepared for the European Championships at Punchestown in Ireland. My team from Japan would also compete but we needed an extra practice horse for Minpei Shirai, so we went shopping. I found a show jumper called Orleans who was not going to make it at the international level; Mr. Shirai liked him, so we brought him back to Fontaine-bleau. The horse proved very willing in the practice sessions so we thought we might try him at a couple of events. They went well, so we continued to compete him. That same year he went to the European Championships!

My experience with flying the horses to Tokyo for the Games in 1964 had been very positive so rather than have the horses bound for Punchestown undergo two sea crossings we decided to fly them. Aer Lingus sent a huge old plane to pick us up at the airport. There were no stalls, just thin plywood kickboards held together with rope. There was no elevator, just a ramp up to the plane that was so steep the horses had a terrible time getting up. One horse, Pitou, absolutely refused to have anything to do with it and twice fell over backward onto the tarmac. In the end, I put the horse onto the horsebox and connected the ramp to the doorway of the plane. This technique proved acceptable to Pitou who walked straight on.

Punchestown was memorable in that I had to coach nine riders from two nations, three of whom spoke little French, but we managed to communicate somehow. We also had the challenge of working with a Technical Delegate ("TD") with whom I had not always had good experiences. Mr. Mayorga of Argentina had been the TD in Tokyo where he had set all the riders on fire when he announced that after the first official course walk the cross-country was closed, and there would be no further walking. I was not hopeful that things would go well.

The steeplechase course at Punchestown racecourse had been in existence for generations and horses had been jumping around the course successfully for almost a century, but Mr. Mayorga insisted that this course was inappropriate and made modifications that he felt would make it more jumpable. This consisted of piling rolls of greenery on the take-off side of all the fences, which made the spread so great that many horses tried to bank the fence and fell. I have never seen so many horses fall on a steeplechase course as did that day.

Britain won the gold medal, Ireland the silver, and France took the team bronze. Pitou and Adjt. Jean-Jacques Guyon placed fourth putting us in a good frame of mind going forward to the Mexico Games the following year. The French team was composed of army and civilian riders as well. I had selected them based on their competitive performances. We had an excellent relationship and knew each other well since we had competed together quite a lot when I was riding myself, and this rapport remained throughout my time as the coach of the French team. I think I can say that we missed each other when I left for the United States.

MEXICO 1968

The preparation for Mexico was going to be critical as the horses and riders would be competing at an altitude of 6,000 feet in Mexico City. We could not have anticipated that the altitude would be the least of our worries. Moreover, I made a serious mistake getting ready for these Olympic Games. To acclimatize the horses to altitude, I took the teams up into the Pyrenees to train. This meant that for the last two to three months leading up to the Olympics they would not be able to compete. Never would I make that mistake again. The horses and riders were missing the fine tuning that only public competition will achieve for you and as a result did not perform in my books to their real potential. And that even goes for Pitou and Jean-Jacques Guyon who eventually won the individual gold medal!

In Mexico, our dressage could have been better and should have been better. The same applied to show jumping also. Of course, no one could have predicted the conditions on the cross-country. The team was very, very fit but they were not competition sharp. Nothing can replace real competition for sharpening up the horses in the lead up to a championship. There is a tendency for riders to think that once picked for the team they are done and that they should not do anything too rigorous because they are frightened that the horse will become unsound. So what happens? They are so afraid that they do nothing and lose their competitive edge. Ideally, I like to have a competition three weeks before the big one, because I believe that is the way to keep them sharp. Leading up to a championship, I apply the rule of three. At the first horse trials, the horses are 60 to 70 percent fit and are blowing a little bit at the end of the cross-country course. The second horse trials they will be 90 percent fit, and by the third, they are 100 percent fit for horse trials. All I have to do then is to give them a few light days, dressage and hacking, then a couple of fast gallop workouts and they are ready to go to the three-day event. That has always worked well for me, at least ever since Mexico!

Once we arrived in Mexico City, we quickly found that there were heavy rainstorms at about the same time every day. The team chefs d'equipe asked the officials to adjust the times of the cross-country to avoid the rain. Just a couple of hours break to allow the water to drain off would have made a considerable difference to the course. We were told this could not be done due to the television coverage that would be going out live. What a mistake!

There were three cross-country competitions in Mexico: the one before the rain, the one during the rain, and the one after the rain. Up to then, the daily downfalls had been quite heavy but nothing compared to the deluge that occurred during the cross-country. A river wound through the course and had to be crossed three times. The water jump had overflowed its banks, and the ditches were transformed into underwater hazards—guess where the edge is if you can! There were expanses of water resembling lakes a foot deep and you could barely see the flags. People from every nation pitched in to help, and we tore down branches from trees to try to mark the take-offs to give the horses something to jump over. Of course, they had no way of knowing whether they were jumping a drop. I have no idea how, but some horses did manage it without falling. Most, though, fell. It was terribly unfair. Some horses fell multiple times, and why they kept going I do not know, but that is the nature of the horse and to abuse it that way is heartbreaking. Why they did not stop that course, I will never know, and I hope that no one ever has to witness that kind of spectacle in this sport again.

The other thing that was notable about Mexico was the steeple-chase course and the roads and tracks. The steeplechase jumps were unnecessarily big, and the roads and tracks were so punishing that most riders had to get off their horses and run beside them going up the hills. Roads and tracks on such steep hills and at 7,000 feet became a feat of endurance in themselves.

I had saved the best and fastest horse until last. The horse, Joburg, had show jumped internationally and was a well-bred Thorough-bred partnered with a superb rider, Jean Sarrazin, himself a well-tuned athlete. They fell once in the river going out but got back together and continued. At the last river crossing at the very end of the course, Joburg fell again. At that point, exhausted and swallowing water, he gave up. The current was dragging him under, and he could not fight it anymore. He was drowning. Many people, mostly riders from other countries, jumped into that torrent of water to save that horse. One of those was the American rider, Kevin Freeman, who I would later come to know well. Kevin helped to keep the horse's head above water until he reached firm footing and could scramble out of the water. This type of selfless action is what makes the sport of eventing so great. This spirit and love for horses transcend all nationalities, and when a horse or rider is in trouble, people pitch in to help, often putting their personal safety to one side. They saved that horse's life that day—at some risk to their own.

While this was happening, farther downstream (or should I say down-torrent!) another drama was playing out. Someone yelled that there was a hand that kept popping up out of the water. It was the rider! Separated from his horse, Jean was being pulled under by the current. People jumped in and saved his life, too. This rider was a fantastic athlete, but as I found out later, he could not swim. I asked him why he didn't tell me that when there were so many river crossings and in those conditions. I can only presume he was too embarrassed to admit it. Of course, the ability to swim had never been a prerequisite for eventing!

Tragically, Jean survived this ordeal only to lose his life in a car accident just before Christmas that same year. Such a dreadful waste of a talented athlete and a fine human being.

The Russians had a brilliant stallion called Paket ridden by Pavel Deyev. Two men presented this horse, one either side of his head, at every horse inspection as he was such a handful, but it made for a very impressive presentation. Pavel and Paket were in the lead going into show jumping on the last day. They could have afforded one rail, which they did not appear to need as they were clear coming to the last two fences on the course. To everyone's complete horror, Pavel jumped the wrong fence. Elimination! Even though this meant my rider, Jean-Jacques Guyon and Pitou (yes the same Pitou who did not want to get on the plane to Ireland) won the gold medal. I felt utter dismay for Pavel. Not only did he lose the gold medal but his team lost a possible medal as well. No one wants to benefit from this type of mistake. We did not see Pavel again for many years and wondered if he had been visiting Siberia!

One other thing came to light in Mexico. The Russians had earphones and were communicating with their coaches while out on the course. After this, the rule got tightened up but up until that time no one had given the use of such equipment much thought. While everyone knew that radios were technically not allowed, there had been no enforcement. However from this point on, that changed.

I had now coached my first Olympic gold medalist (not counting my juniors!). I hoped it wouldn't be my last.

The system by which the French equestrian teams were managed at that time was cumbersome and complicated—something I had quickly determined when I first took up the position in 1965. Too many parties were involved in the production of teams. First, the Federation of course, then the Army maintained the stable and the horses, and then the Ministry of Agriculture from whence the funding came. Each wanted a strong voice in the proceedings, and there were endless meetings. I had explained my frustrations with this set-up to the Federation, telling them that I did not want to continue like this and that I had drawn up a plan for a more efficient process. I had been disappointed that no action had been taken and had begun to lose patience. Before leaving for Mexico, I had once again addressed the issue and said that if changes were not made by the time we returned from Mexico, I would resign. Upon my return, I went to the Federation to see where things stood. "Oh, we didn't have time!" was the answer.

"You have had three years, and nothing is going to happen now in time for the new Olympic cycle," I said. I resigned right then and finally went into private business as originally planned.

7

COMING TO AMERICA

In the United States, meanwhile, the great Bert de Némethy was the coach of the US Olympic Show Jumping Team. In the mid-sixties, he recommended a colleague of his, Stephan von Visy, from the Hungarian Cavalry to coach the US Three-Day Eventing Team for the Mexico Olympics. Stephan was appointed to the job but for whatever reason, the arrangement did not work out and Major Joe Lynch, the future Director of the Morven Park Equestrian Institute, stepped in on a short-term contract to coach the team. He did well in Mexico because the United States won the team silver medal. When Joe's contract ended, Michael Page put forward my name as a candidate to take over the team coaching job. Michael had taken a course as an international student at the Cadre Noir in Saumur when I was responsible for eventing, and I am pretty sure that when he rode his first event ever in the south of France it was under my tutelage.

And so it was that in the fall of 1969, I received a call from Commandant Jean St. Fort-Paillart, a Frenchman who lived in California and who coached Patricia Galvin in dressage. Patricia was the daughter of John Galvin, a prominent California businessman and she was aiming for a berth on the US Dressage Team at the 1972 Munich Olympic

Games. As I spoke little English and Whitney Stone, then president of the USET, spoke no French he asked Jean to contact me to see if I was interested in coaching the US Eventing Team. Mr. Stone was heading to Paris for the famous French horse race, l'Arc de Triomphe, and so I arranged to meet with him to begin negotiations. My wife Madeleine spoke fluent English as not only did she graduate from university with an English degree, she had also spent a year in Kansas and so was a very able interpreter at that first meeting in Paris. Mr. Stone then invited me to come to New York that November to attend the National Horse Show where we would discuss the position in further detail. Meg Plum of Hamilton Farms in Massachusetts, and whose parents owned Michael Page's ride Foster, came along to New York as interpreter, and at that second meeting, I accepted the offer of a one-year contract to coach the US Team. Mr. Stone promised that if I didn't like it after one year, or vice versa, the team didn't like me, then they would ship me back to France. Now came the challenge—I had two months to brush up my English.

GLADSTONE

I arrived in Gladstone, New Jersey in January 1970. I was to get everything set up for my family to join me later. Upon arrival at Team Headquarters, I was heartened to find that an organization very similar to the process I had suggested to the French Federation was already in place, and felt sure I would be able to work with that type of structure.

At Gladstone, I shared the riding facilities and an office with Bert de Némethy. It was evident that Bert was disappointed that his friend Stephan von Visy did not work out as coach of the Three-Day Team, and, of course, whoever was to succeed him was not going to be receiving the welcome that one would hope. However, soon after my arrival, Bert was to leave for Europe with the jumping team so I would have some time to settle in.

There had been no eventing activities at Gladstone since the 1968 Olympics in Mexico: no tack, no grooms, and no horses. Jack Burton loaned the first horse that came to the team, and I was grooming him as well as cleaning up—by myself I might add—the downstairs barn, which had been closed for two years. I also rehabilitated three team horses, Plain Sailing, Chalan, and Foster, who had been turned out since Mexico.

My real challenge, though, was to find riders. Out of the international riders, only Mike Plumb, Jim Wofford, and Kevin Freeman were still active and interested. Michael Page had retired from eventing and was concentrating on the horse show business.

A competition calendar did not exist. The United States had seen quite a surge in eventing beginning with the first event in Tennessee in 1953. Three-day events and Olympic selection trials were held in a number of places, including the Broadmoor in Colorado and Pebble Beach in California, but when I arrived in 1970, there were no Advanced horse trials and just two Intermediate three-day events scheduled in the entire United States. I went to one of them. There were only three starters: Charlotte Robson, Mike Bowman, and Stewart Treviranus. The other I attended was in California and run by Dick Collins at Pebble Beach. With so few competitions on the calendar and those spread over three thousand miles, I had my work cut out!

Not only did I need riders but I thought the system of having just a handful of riders waiting to find out which team horse they were going to be given to ride at the next international competition was just not healthy. So, I contacted one of the few people I knew, Meg Plum of Hamilton, Massachusetts, and asked her if it was possible to organize a gathering of interested riders to be considered for the three-day event team. I then went to Hamilton to work with the dozen or so riders she had invited, one of whom was a young man called Bruce Davidson. Bert had mentioned to me that he saw

Bruce while he was conducting screening trials for the jumping team and felt Bruce had a lot of talent but might be more interested in eventing.

Out of that group, I selected Bruce, the two Powers brothers, Jim and David, and Marshall and Lendon Gray. They were all invited to go to Gladstone for further evaluation. Lendon Gray was more interested in dressage and did not stay, but Bruce, the two Powers boys, and Marshall were asked to stay full time for training. Upon filling out the forms for amateur status, Marshall Gray, with her great integrity, wrote down that she had received compensation for helping at a Pony Club camp. I was advised straight away by the USET President at the time, George Merck, that she was a professional and as such had to leave for home the following day. In the few short weeks Marshall had been at Gladstone, I realized what a great person she was, extremely dedicated and conscientious, very knowledgeable, and excellent at taking care of the horses. I was not prepared to send her home. I also needed stable personnel, so I offered Marshall the job of barn manager and offered to help her with her horse if she would stay. She gladly accepted, and that was the start of a tremendous partnership. Marshall set a very high standard of stable management, which carried through the years even after she had to leave the team for serious health reasons.

When Bert came back from Europe a couple of months later, he saw Marshall in the stables and asked me what she was doing at the team. I said that I had hired her as barn manager and was very pleased with her work. Bert responded in a very excited and emotional way saying that he had tried having girls in the barn, and they did not work out, he didn't want them there, and he told me to tell Marshall to go home. I very calmly said, "Bert, I am sorry, but I hired her and she is going to stay." Bert was furious saying that he had been here for many years, and that was that. I then had to take a stand and said, "When I was hired by Mr. Stone, President of the

USET, I was never at any time told that I was going to work under Mr. de Némethy's control and direction. I respect the way you are handling your job as jumping coach, but I have every intention of managing and directing my own coaching job and will make my own decisions in the interest of the team."

A few months later, Bert said to me privately, "Jack, you were right about Marshall, she is a great girl." Only a man like Bert could say this. After our altercation, we became good friends. Often I would ride his horses when he was away, and he helped me if I had a problem with a horse and its show jumping. I will always think of him with great fondness.

PLANTING THE SEEDS

While I was in Hamilton, Meg Plum introduced me to a man who was to become a lifelong friend and colleague. Neil Ayer had just become the president of the US Combined Training Association. He and his wife Helen owned Ledyard Farm in Wenham, Massachusetts, and the encounter between Neil and myself was the trigger point for the development of eventing in the United States due to the common interest we both enthusiastically shared. Neil asked me how things were going and if there was anything I needed. I told him we needed more competitions at all levels, but especially at the advanced and international levels. "Okay," he said. "I'll take care of it." Being the man that he was, he immediately set about making that happen. He created the competitions, and I created the riders to compete in them. It was then that the seeds of what was to become the 1973 Ledyard Farm International Three-Day Event were germinated.

The show jumping team's set-up at Gladstone was a little different from mine. Bert had the upper-level stalls and did not have any riders in residence. The horses were owned by the team, and the riders came when it was getting close to the Olympics or other top international competitions, and it was simply a matter of choosing which horse each would ride. It had been similar with three-day eventing. Plumb, Freeman, and Page all rode team horses. Jim Wofford rode his mother's Kilkenny but at this time there were no other riders in contention for a team place.

With the 1972 Munich Olympics looming, I had a huge hill to climb, and I found out what pressure was all about quickly. I had great hopes for Bruce Davidson, but he was so young, and there was so much to teach him. Another problem needed solving: there were not enough horses. As I already mentioned, I had access to three old team horses and brought them back to Gladstone for training. One was Chalan who had been on the Team in Mexico. To my horror, Chalan tested positive for Equine Infectious Anemia (EIA), which is transmitted by mosquitoes from horse to horse and for which there is no cure. While it did not affect him, he was a carrier, and he could have put many horses at risk. I would have been in awful trouble if I had kept him alive. There was nothing to do but put him down. We did not want to panic the neighboring stables, so we told them that he was an older horse with a great career behind him and was not quite sound. The kindest thing to do was put him down. Patrick Lynch was very attached to the horse and wanted to kill me for that decision. If he had simply been lame Patrick would have nursed him to health and then taken care of him in his retirement. With EIA that is simply not possible, so I had to tell him the truth, and he was then able to accept it. But, it was an awful blow. Now I needed horses more than ever.

With these young riders now training at Gladstone, I wondered how the experienced team riders would receive them. I found that they were happy to let me look around at the up and coming riders and train them because they knew that I would still call on them to ride for the team in Munich.

But the lack of horses worried me. Meg Plum and her family came to the rescue by sending me Foster. He was getting older, and I oriented him more on dressage and he rose to the occasion. I was able to get him going in piaffe and passage and put the young riders on him to teach them how it felt.

A call to that most generous of all supporters Ray Firestone resulted in the return of Plain Sailing to the team. I was given a couple of other horses, and now we were in business, but with Bruce beginning to look like a future champion, we needed a class horse for him to compete.

A friend of Bert de Némethy, Gabor Foltenyi, told Bert about a possible event horse in Ohio. Since this man was a good friend of Bert's I trusted him and asked if the horse could come to Gladstone for a week for us to try. The owner, Mr. Lewis, kindly agreed, and this big, bay horse duly arrived. I wanted to keep him long enough to be sure that if any medications had been administered, they would wear off, and we would get an exact look at the horse's ability. On first glance, he was not the ideal type being very big and solid, a typical well-boned Irish horse. We did not know his breeding, and he had been through so many hands that his history was blurred. He was sound but green. I rode him as well as Bruce and thought there was something very promising about him. The price was fairly reasonable, and I suggested to Bruce that he tell his father to go ahead and have him vetted.

I had an appointment on the day of the vetting and so wasn't present when the team vet examined the horse and took X-rays. In his opinion, the X-rays were not good enough, and he failed the horse. Bruce found out that a van was going back to Ohio that night and put the horse on it. When I got back to the barn, I asked where Irish Cap was, and Bruce told me what had happened. I couldn't believe it. We had had the horse for a week; we had jumped him, and he seemed entirely sound. "I want that horse back," I told Bruce. Bruce said his father wouldn't buy him if he didn't pass the vet and I told him that I would take full responsibility. Finally, Bruce got the horse shipped back, and three years later they became World Champions. But I am getting ahead of myself.

Now we had a larger pool of riders and thanks to Neil we had some competitions to enter. Added to that, the team of horses was growing. Suddenly, the senior riders started to pay attention. I had been telling them all year, any time you want to come and train at the team just let me know and no one had knocked on my door. When the younger riders in team training started enjoying some success, the other riders thought they had better take some action as these youngsters might upstage them and so the phone started ringing. Now I was able to start team training in earnest.

It was about this time that my less than perfect English got me into a bit of trouble. A competition was to be held at what is now the Fair Hill Natural Resource Area in Elkton, Maryland. I had spent the day at the property designing the course and helping to build the fences and was pretty dirty. My hosts, the Du Pont family, were holding a party that night, and when I returned to the house, the festivities had already started. I announced to all gathered that I would just run upstairs to take a "douche" and would be right down. I had no idea why that caused such hilarity until it was explained to me later, at which point my face turned a suitable shade of beet red! I was to continue to entertain many more partygoers as the years went on.

8

I Meet the Queen and the US Team Becomes "A Threat to Be Reckoned With"

My first team coaching assignment for the United States was the 1972 Munich Olympic Games, and it was not going to be an easy one. Due to an outbreak of Venezuelan Equine Encephalitis (VEE), a mandatory six-month quarantine was instituted, which meant with the Olympics scheduled for October, all horses had to be in Europe by May 1st. The USET was faced with shipping all short-listed horses in all three Olympic disciplines almost immediately and keeping them housed and in training for that entire time. That posed a huge expense as well as a logistical nightmare and meant that we did not have the comfort of making adequate arrangements.

We took five riders, twelve horses and all the grooms to England in time to meet the quarantine deadlines. We needed the extra horses for the riders to train on and also to act as replacements should any of the horses on the first list go lame, as with the quarantine restrictions we could not simply call home and have another one sent over. My pick for the first list was Foster, the former ride of the now retired Michael Page, Free and Easy, Kilkenny, Good Mixture, and Plain Sailing.

In addition to the more experienced riders Kevin Freeman, Mike Plumb, and Jim Wofford, we took the two younger riders Bruce

Davidson and Jim Powers. This was quite an accomplishment for these two young men who in two years had gone from having no eventing experience to speak of, to riding on an Olympic team. In fact, Bruce had not known what a diagonal was when he first came to me. He quickly learned! But that was the key to Bruce; his willingness to learn, coupled with his innate talent, made teaching him a very satisfying experience as you would see him improve right before your eyes. Jim also worked hard to achieve his goals and the two deserved their places on the team.

Quarantine and the Queen

The horses were taken straight to a quarantine facility on a government-approved farm for the required period of quarantine. They were tested, and one horse tested positive, so all the horses stayed there and were not released in time to compete at an event taking place that weekend at Windsor on Her Majesty the Queen's land, so, I decided to make use of the time and take the riders to watch. At the event, Princess Anne came to me and told me that the Queen wished to speak with me. When we met, she said, "Mr. Le Goff, I am sorry that your riders cannot participate at the event, but even the Queen of England cannot interfere with the veterinary regulations." I thought it was very kind of her to take the time to speak with me.

The next week we were told that the test results were wrong, and the horse was fine, so we were released from quarantine. Mike Bullen worked for Peden, the largest horse transportation company in the world. He had worked for the USET and was also a British event rider. I had hired Mike to transport the horses to England, and now he offered to arrange for us to go to his sister's farm in Brockenhurst in Hampshire. The farm is right on the edge of the ancient New Forest where King Henry VIII used to hunt and which is famous for its New Forest ponies, one of England's most popular native breeds. So we went there, trained, and managed to fit in some competitions.

Mike also arranged for the riders and me to stay at a rather fancy hotel and the grooms at another perfectly acceptable hotel. Our stay there did not last long because the fancy hotel was quite expensive and the farm was not appropriate for training event horses because it did not provide a place to gallop so I made the decision to move the team to a more suitable facility.

The riders were on a per diem, which meant they were free to buy their food up to a certain dollar amount per day, and after that, they were on their own. The hotel, as hotels in England did at that time, would put out fruit, cookies, and other tidbits on the dining table before dinner. One day the manager of the fancy hotel took me aside and told me that the maids were refusing to clean the bedrooms because they were in such a dreadful state and the maitre d' was furious because all the fruit and cookies had been stolen before the guests sat down to dinner at night. The hotel management stopped putting out these pre-dinner treats, which drove the riders to be more creative in their attempts to assuage their hunger while saving money. One night one of our hungrier riders found his way to the kitchens to raid the refrigerator when an employee of the hotel began his night rounds. To avoid being caught our rider hid in the broom closet, like something out of one of those farces that are so popular in London theaters. There was no doubt about it—it was time for us to go!

The riders could not be away from their homes and businesses for the entire quarantine period and left for the States after the spring season. The grooms and I had to take full responsibility for all the horses and keep them exercised and in training until the riders returned for the fall season. Once the riders left for the home, it fell to me to keep the horses ridden and schooled every day. I never had a day off and often felt alone. The riders and grooms had each other and would often get together socially. While I was on excellent terms with them, as a coach I did not get involved too much and spent many evenings simply planning the next day's work and taking care of the accounting.

Patrick Lynch was a mainstay of the team and during those early years was with me on every trip. He started off as a groom, moved to traveling head man and eventually became the farm manager at the USET headquarters in Gladstone, which was wonderful for him but it meant our days of traveling together would one day be over. At this time, we were also lucky to have Marshall Gray travel with us and she continued to impress me with her dedication to the horses and her attention to detail. Overall, I was very blessed with my team of grooms.

CULTURE SHOCK

One thing that became very apparent to me during this trip was the difference between the European educational system, and that of the Americans. Traveling to England and France with the younger riders was an eye-opener. Once when driving down a street in London, a rider asked me how old a particular building was. "Oh, about 1,000 years old!" I said. He was aghast, having no idea that a building could stand that long. There was little knowledge of European history, and I blame the education system in America. Even today, most students know very little about world history and geography and in truth, few know very little about what is going on outside of the United States. The younger riders knew nothing about the Iron Curtain or the Cold War. Few knew any other language than English, which was fine in England but in France and Germany, it put them at a disadvantage. How can you appreciate a culture if you don't speak the language, or even attempt to learn it?

The five riders, most of them college graduates, went to Europe and experienced cultural shock. Summers in Europe were not that hot and the old houses and stores in England, France, and Germany didn't have air conditioning. They couldn't understand that. European houses have multiple bedrooms, sometimes eight, nine, or more, and only one bathroom. That was unheard of to these riders. I had to spend a lot of time explaining to them that European countries are not third world countries.

So, with the riders back home in the States, it was left to me to keep the horses in work. One day, I was hacking Kilkenny out and got lost. We rode around for ages and finally got to where I could see the stables, but there was no way to get there without jumping a post and rail fence about 4 feet 3 inches high. Kilkenny did not have a good reputation for jumping verticals but by this time I had been lost for about two hours and decided I was not going to ride around trying to find my way out of the woods. There was nothing else to be done—I would jump the fence. I took Kilkenny up to it and showed him it, went back 10 strides, turned, picked up the canter and rode him at the fence. He jumped it in superb style, and we went home to the stables. I would not, however, recommend this type of activity for everyone, especially not when alone.

The social life was non-existent in Yorkshire. The stables were in a small village called Bolton where there was only one shop that sold the basics: toothpaste, cigarettes, hand soap, and little else. The shop was a private home owned and operated by an old lady. I recall she had one tooth left in her upper jaw. She wore shoes with straw in them and plastic for socks. But after three long months on my own, she started to look like Marilyn Monroe to me!

There were quite a few racing stables around, and we were able to take advantage of some superb gallops, which helped with the fitness and conditioning. The hacking was beautiful as well and at that time, you could get out on the country roads and walk for hours. Today you would be taking your life in your hands with the amount of traffic there is, not to mention the speed at which it all travels! All of this helped us prepare a team that was more than fit and ready to take on the Olympic track in Munich.

THE MUNICH OLYMPICS

The riders returned to England in time for some intensive days of training, following which the team headed to Munich for the Olympics. There, every morning, we had to take a bus at daybreak to our training facilities, which were quite a distance away from the Olympic Village. That specific morning, the bus was not at its usual place. After waiting a few minutes, I went to inquire at the gate, and a German security person told me that there was a significant problem inside the Olympic Village. He did not want to be more specific. He said that our bus was just outside. On the bus, the radio was on, and between the radio and driver I found out that there was a tragic situation developing in the Village. We went on through our usual schedule of training and as the day went on we learned more details about the taking of hostages. When we drove back that evening to the Village, our building was next to the Israeli building, and we could clearly see the terrorists with their faces hidden with masks and armed with guns out on the balcony. Obviously, the situation and atmosphere in the Village changed drastically from a usually joyful crowd of athletes from different nations, races, and religions. All the faces became stern, looking down. That atmosphere reflected the tragedy unfolding before our eyes. We learned that the hostages had been killed. A few days later a service took place in memory of those innocent victims, which will never be forgotten by anyone there.

The attitude of the athletes reflected the horror and gravity of the situation which dealt a shocking blow to the Olympic spirit. Poor Baron de Coubertin must have been turning in his grave as it certainly was not what he had in mind when he revived the modern Olympic Games.

Nevertheless, the Games had to go on, and our riders did well. The US team was made up of Bruce Davidson and Plain Sailing, Kevin Freeman and Good Mixture, Mike Plumb and Free and Easy, and Jim Wofford and Kilkenny. Jim Powers was the reserve rider on Foster, never an easy position to be in as you have to be ready to ride right up until the first vet inspection and then if all goes well with the other four horses you do not get to ride at all. Jim handled himself admirably even though his disappointment must have been great.

My team strategy was to have the most experienced horse and rider as the first one out for the team on the cross-country course. This is not necessarily the best horse, but it has to be an experienced rider who can get an accurate reading of how the course is riding and pass that on to the others back in the start box. I always tried to keep the fastest horse until last because if you have an experienced horse that only has one speed and you put him last, you are at a disadvantage. A fast horse can go slower but a slow horse cannot go faster. You may need that speed to clinch the performance for the team.

The riders always had to walk the cross-country course first, preferably as a group, without me. I walked alone. Then we would walk together and after that, they would go out again on their own. The last walk should always be done completely alone. The most difficult thing I had to get into some rider's heads was to walk the course as if it was the only time they would be able to walk it. I didn't want them running around just getting a first impression, but I wanted them to concentrate and envision how they would ride it. A walk simply to get a first impression is a wasted walk.

I learned this from my experience in Rome. A few days before the Olympics, I injured an ankle quite severely and absolutely could not walk. As there were no motorized vehicles, I had to do my course walk on crutches. Both the steeplechase and cross-country courses were much longer than today, and anyone who has ever tried to walk with crutches will understand why I knew I wouldn't be able to make it around the course three times! I knew that one walk would have to be it. I might get back to a couple of the combinations, but I would not be walking the entire course again. That was when I learned that you could ride a course after walking it only one time if you had total concentration. I required my riders to think that same way.

The team strategy was based on receiving the best possible information while the endurance test was developing. Back in 1972, there were no portable phones and the rules, severely tightened after Mexico, did not allow radios. The teams had a pretty good communication system, called the "spy system," which consisted of "spotters" spread out over the course who would send information back with runners. One person would gather all the information, analyze it, and then bring the results to me in the vet box. The first rider out could not benefit from this at all, the second has something to work with, but the third and fourth riders go out armed with a wealth of information on the best way to ride the course.

In Munich, the British employed the same system. Lord Hugh Russell, who with his wife Rosemary ran the Wylie event in England, approached me in the vet box with a message. Hugh and I were good friends, and Hugh had a great sense of humor. "One of the American runners gave this to the British by mistake," he said. With a gleam in his eye, he continued, "I did take the liberty of having a peek at it, hope you don't mind!"

Funny enough, the coaches and chefs d'equipe of the different nations were all pretty good friends. Bill Lithgow, a special friend of mine, was the chef d'equipe for the British. There is a spirit of sportsmanship that is so evident amongst the eventing teams that friendships and personal relationships rise above the heat of competition. Oh don't get me wrong, each still has a fiery determination to see their team win, but at the day's end, we all are still, for the most part, good friends. And when the chips are down, and a horse and rider are in trouble, as we saw in Mexico, national pride goes by the wayside, and we are just a human and an animal in need, and that transcends all national barriers.

My opinion of the course in Munich was that it was a very valid Olympic cross-country and looked quite polished compared to those at previous Olympic Games. In hindsight, it was a forerunner of the type of courses we would see for the next 30 years.

I was very proud of my first US Olympic team for bringing home our first Olympic team medal. It did not matter that it was silver and not gold. I determined that we would change the color of the medal in the not too distant future.

Fifi Coles, the editor of the *USCTA News* at that time, wrote some very nice things about my coaching and touched me when she said, "Under Le Goff a new aura of respect and understanding developed for eventing in horse circles throughout this country. In England, and in all Europe, 'the Americans' were, and will continue to be held in new esteem...an imminent threat to be reckoned with in just a year and a half at the World Championships in England." We all hoped, and none more than me, that she was right.

9

THE SYSTEM

Shortly after we returned from Munich, I started a post-Olympic year system of a series of screening trials based on existing competitions that would help me pinpoint those riders with the potential to be put in training with hopefully the further potential of becoming international riders. The purpose of this system was to help me find new and talented riders, and if they happened to have a good horse, that was a plus. The riders had to compete at the Preliminary level or above. They also had to let me know by letter that they wanted to be considered for the team. I was most interested in their way of riding, not their results. At the end of the trials, I ended up with about 30 to 40 riders on the list who had potential. They were invited to team headquarters for a training session as well as further evaluation. Each session was a minimum of 10 days to three weeks, depending on the circumstances, and around 10 to 12 riders in each session. At the end of this talent search process, I usually picked four riders that would commit themselves to be in training from then on until the next Olympic Games. They would then start full-time training with me every day. Hopefully, they would come with one or two horses, but if they had no horses the Team always had a few that could be used to train the riders.

There were no guarantees that these four riders automatically had a berth on the team. Selection trials would take place before each Pan American Games, Olympic Games, and Worlds. Competitions would be selected to act as selection trials. Obviously, the selection trials were open to anyone who wanted to represent the United States. That included the old team riders, the young riders in training, and anybody else. At the end of the selection process, a short list would be established, and riders would go into training at the appropriate places and in time for the major upcoming event.

This was the system I used to develop team riders for the next three Olympics. Over 12 years it successfully produced 12 to 14 top international riders. The United States ended up having enough riders available to represent the country at the Olympics and other international events such as the World Championships and Lexington 1978. In fact, in 1978 the system had produced enough riders to provide four team riders plus eight individual riders for the Lexington event. The system worked.

A NEED FOR COMPETITION

Another problem we faced in 1973 was the lack of international events where we could evaluate our performance against the top riders from other countries. You can be extremely successful at home against your peers week after week, but unless you occasionally test yourself against the best in the world, it is hard to get a measure of your competitiveness on the international scene.

True to his word, as he always was, Neil Ayer stepped up the preparation for his promised international three-day event and in October 1973 the first FEI CCI on US soil was held at his Ledyard Farm in Wenham, Massachusetts. Neil invited riders from England, Ireland, France, and Germany. Ireland and France sent three riders each and Britain sent 13. Some of the greatest names in British eventing made the trip. Three members of the gold medal team from

Munich, Mary Gordon Watson (with her brilliant 1970 reigning World Champion, Cornishman V), Bridget Parker, and my good friend Mark Phillips were among the British contingent. Sue Hatherly, also of Britain, won the event with Mike Plumb taking second and third. It is exciting to see Sue Hatherly, who is now Sue Benson, become one of Britain's foremost course designers and her work on the courses at the Bramham CCI3* in Yorkshire and at Boekelo in the Netherlands are an example of her talent.

Some other, soon to be prominent eventing names came onto the scene in 1973. US riders Don Sachey, Beth Perkins, and Denny Emerson all started to make their presence felt throughout that summer.

The list of officials and volunteers for Ledyard was a who's who of the eventing world. Donald Thackeray, Jack Burton, Bengt Ljungquist, Jack Fritz, Mrs. Igor Presnikoff, and Hans Moeller, Bill Steinkraus, Paul Wimert, and others all worked to make the event a success. Sheila Wilcox, winner of Badminton in 1957, 1958, and 1959, came from England as did Eileen Thomas who did all the scoring. Eileen came back the following year to work for Neil at the USCTA becoming the Executive Director of the association in 1978.

Two very famous event horses, both of which I had the pleasure of working with, were given very moving retirement ceremonies at Ledyard. One was Kilkenny, one of only three horses to have competed in three Olympic Games and two World Championships. He had competed for Ireland with Tommy Brennan in the Tokyo Olympics and the 1966 World Championships at Burghley (team gold) before being sold to Jim Wofford who went on to win two Olympic team silver medals (Mexico and Munich), and the individual bronze medal at the Punchestown World Championships in 1970. Imagine more than 12 years at the top of the international game and he retired sound—what an achievement! Also retiring was Foster who had competed in Mexico again with Michael Page and who went on to be the reserve horse with Jim Powers in Munich. The retirement of these two horses though meant that there would be a big hole to fill going into the World Championship year of 1974, and we needed some of the young horses and riders to capitalize on the promise they had shown so far if we were to be in contention.

Another significant arrangement was made after "Ledyard '73." Forrester A. Clark donated part of the old Clark estate in South Hamilton, Massachusetts, to the USET and the old stables, barns, and houses were developed into the new USET Training Center. South Hamilton would soon become home to my family and me and was to remain so for 18 years to come.

Tad Coffin and Bally Cor

The screening trials of 1973 helped me identify some prospective international riders and one of these was the talented teenager, Tad Coffin. I was so impressed that I invited Tad to join the team at Gladstone.

Dr. Charles Reid had bred one of his mares to the steeplechase stallion Cormac, and the result was a dark bay mare, Bally Cor. Harden Crawford III and his wife Ailsa had purchased a 50 percent share of the mare and Denny Crawford had started her off in her eventing career. While Bally Cor did not immediately catch the eye as a potential international horse, she more than made up for this with one of the biggest hearts in the game. I approached Harden Crawford and asked him to consider loaning Bally Cor to the USET for the duration of her competitive career. He very kindly agreed and made possible the partnership of Tad Coffin and Bally Cor. It proved to be one of the best moves I ever made and produced possibly the most successful eventing combination of the 1970's.

I planned two selection trials for the first half of 1974: the Middletown Pony Club Horse Trials in Middletown, Delaware, on May 12 and the Essex Horse Trials in Far Hills, New Jersey, on June 1. Both produced some exciting results. Don Sachey and Landmark won Mid-

1. I'm eleven years old and ready for my First Communion.
Photo by Marie Ange Le Goff.

2. Riding for Vladimir Hall, I'm led around the paddock on Gros Buisson prior to winning the grand steeplechase and cross-country at Saumur in 1950.

3. The Riding Masters of Saumur line up for a photograph in 1952. I'm on the far right. *Photo by Hervé Blanchaud.*

4. Barbot and I perform the croupade, Saumur 1954. *Photo by Hervé Blanchaud.*

5. Lining up for the start of the Cadre Noir cross-country race, I'm second from right.

6. Prize-giving after I won the Army track race in Saumur.

7. Riding Laurier to third place at Burghley in 1963. The event was won by Capt. Harry Freeman-Jackson on St. Finbarr. Shelagh Kesler and Lochinvar were tied with Laurier at the end of the competition and actually finished on the same score, but when the tie was broken, Laurier was placed third. With the fastest cross-country round Laurier was closest to the optimum time which would have given him 2nd place today.

8. Image and me helping the French Team to a bronze medal at the Rome Olympics in 1960.

9. Jumping as a civilian in the Four-Year-Old Championships on Indeci.

10, 11. On course with Image, Rome Olympics, 1960. *Photos by Jean Bridel.*

12. Jumping the open ditch in Rome. As you can see, a horse before me had sadly died when he missed his footing at the poorly built ditch and fallen. The officials simply moved the flags and kept the competition going. I had to do some quick thinking when I arrived at the approach to the ditch having planned my route for the right-hand side. Image was amazing. She focused on the question and was not distracted by the activity off to her side. This would never be allowed to happen in this day and age (see p. 182).

13. Image made only one mistake on the entire course in Rome. She misjudged the big oxer over a ditch right at the beginning of the course and landed on her belly. The obstacle in this photo was the very next fence, a double road crossing with rails in front. She could have cleared it or banked it; she chose the cautious route and you can see her putting down on the top of the bank. I could hear her saying, "I got it wrong once and I am not doing that again!" She was foot perfect the rest of the way.

14. Image preparing to receive her well-deserved team bronze medal. Unfortunately, only one medal was awarded per team so we didn't get to keep it. Only three riders were invited to the podium: the rider with the dropped score, no matter how good, was excluded from the ceremony.
Photo by Alix Coleman.

15. The teams lined up for the medal presentation on the Plaza de Sienna where the show jumping for eventing took place. Note individual gold medalist Bill Roycroft (fifth from the left) holding his hand in front of him. That was the broken arm in a sling!

16. People won't believe this is me because I am so darn thin. Coeur de Lilas competed and won the French National Three-Day Event Championships with me in 1956 and went on to race successfully winning one race by 20 lengths.

17. During the Algerian war, I was an intelligence officer in the French army. This was because I spoke Arabic fluently. Here I am with some of the Arab commandoes from my unit. Standing to my left is the radio guy, the only native Frenchman. *Photo by Jean-François Renard.*

18. Off to war! Here I am in the Atlas Mountains during the Algerian war in 1961. There is snow on the ground and we were living in tents until we could get a fort built. *Photo by Jean-François Renard.*

19. We were stationed in this old Foreign Legion outpost on the high plateau of the Atlas Mountains. My unit was stationed here for about a year before moving into the mountains.

20. My brother Pierre (left) was in another squadron stationed 200 kilometers away and we met on very rare occasions. Here, on one of those, we had put on a horse show and we are walking around the warm-up prior to jumping. My horse was an Anglo-Arab Barb and he and I together won a couple of international speed classes at 1.40m. *Photo by Jean-François Renard.*

21. My favorite, Image—a most unlikely event horse by a trotter stallion out of an Anglo-Arab mare. She was the smartest horse I ever knew and never had a stop on cross-country. This was taken on my return from Algeria. I wanted to get her going again for the Tokyo Games, but it wasn't to be.

22. Pitou and Jean-Jacques Guyon puts in a clear show jumping round to win the individual gold medal in Mexico.

23. My Olympic coaching assignment, 1968 Mexico.

24. Pitou again. The show jumping team wanted Pitou for the Olympics prior to Mexico but the eventing team prevailed. I resigned as coach after Mexico and Pitou became a top show jumper with Commandant Pierre Durand.

25. My first United States Team. L–R: Bruce Davidson and Plain Sailing; Jim Wofford and Kilkenny; Kevin Freeman and Good Mixture; Jim Powers (reserve) and Foster; Mike Plumb and Free and Easy. *Photo by Fifi Coles.*

26. The gold medal team at the 1974 World Championships at Burghley: HRH Prince Philip, the Duke of Edinburgh presenting the prizes to Mike Plumb on Good Mixture; Bruce Davidson on Irish Cap; Denny Emerson on Victor Dakin; and Don Sachey on Plain Sailing. *Photo by Werner Ernst.*

27. Tad Coffin, one of my star pupils. *Photo by Nancy Shackleton.*

dletown and Roger Haller and Golden Griffin won the Essex Trials. Other soon-to-be-famous names came to the fore at Middletown. Caroline Treviranus rode Cajun into third, Beth Perkins and Furtive were sixth, while Bally Cor and Tad Coffin were a very commendable eighth just ahead of Denny Emerson and Victor Dakin. Beth Perkins bettered Furtive's score at Essex by placing second to Roger Haller. Denny Emerson moved Victor Dakin up a notch with a good third place, while Landmark and Don Sachey had to settle for sixth this time around. We were starting to see some consistent performances, which were real confidence boosters.

Meanwhile, Bruce Davidson had married Carol Hannum, and both were training in England at Wylie, the home of Lord and Lady Hugh Russell. Both Carol and Bruce were entered in the Badminton Horse Trials on Paddy and Irish Cap respectively. Unfortunately, Paddy was eliminated on the cross-country, but Irish Cap and Bruce maintained their form and finished in third place. The event was won by a pretty good guy called Mark Phillips who rode his mother-in-law's (Queen Elizabeth) Columbus.

The team was planning to go to England early to get the horses and riders tuned up for Burghley with a couple of British events. Following the two selection trials, we had quite a good list of horses and riders from which to choose. The Selection Committee of Neil Ayer, Jack Burton, Jack Fritz, and I put together a short list of Tad Coffin, Denny Emerson, Lornie Forbes, Roger Haller, Beth Perkins, Mike Plumb, Don Sachey, and Caroline Treviranus and invited them to come up to Hamilton to train. Bruce Davidson was named to the list but was given the opportunity to stay with Irish Cap in England where he would await the arrival of his teammates.

On August 1, we shipped 14 horses and six riders to Wylie to begin our challenge for the World Championships. At the top of the list were the horses that had shown most consistency in the competitions at home. Added to this was their soundness. The horses with those criteria as well as having the best records and deemed most likely to complete the competition were the ones we selected. Apart from Mike Plumb who had represented the US in every Olympic Games since Rome in 1960 and Bruce who had made his debut in Munich, the riders were all newcomers to the international scene. Denny Emerson, Beth Perkins, Don Sachey, and Caroline Treviranus joined Bruce in England for the final preparations, working on the technical aspects of riding as well as the conditioning and the fitness of the horses.

THE 1974 WORLD CHAMPIONSHIPS

Back in Munich, the British individual and team gold medalist, Richard Meade, who was more "British" than most Britons, asked me how I was getting along in the States. I told him that everything was going very well. "How is your English?" he asked. "My English is coming along very well Richard, but God you have a funny accent!" I replied. Then he said, "Jack, it would be very good for the sport if some country, other than Britain, could win one of the big ones someday." To which I replied smilingly, "Richard, you can count on me to make that happen."

Now I had to put my money where my mouth was. The British were obviously the hot favorites, and everyone expected them to take the gold again just as they had done at Punchestown in the 1970 Worlds and again in Munich at the Olympic Games. The night before Burghley started the organizers put on a fun evening of activities, which included a donkey race for the chefs d'equipe and some of the riders. Bill Lithgow, the British chef, fell off his donkey and broke seven ribs and spent the entire weekend in the hospital. While I had great sympathy for my friend Bill, I had to ask myself if this was a sign that luck was not with the British this time around.

After walking the course, I decided that the four men Denny, Mike, Don, and Bruce should ride for the team, and the two girls, Beth and

Caroline, would ride as individuals. This had absolutely nothing to do with gender as I have always believed that girls, provided they had suitable horses, could compete successfully against the men. Beth had had an accident while setting up the horses in the temporary stabling. She was carrying a heavy trunk and had slipped, dropping the trunk and breaking two bones in her foot. Nevertheless, being the resilient young woman she was there was no stopping her riding.

Bruce and Irish Cap rose to the occasion in the dressage and performed better than they ever had before and at the end of the day stood in second place to the Russian Vladimir Laniugin on the stallion, Tost. The team as a whole was second to the Germans with the French behind in third. The British were in fourth.

The cross-country was big; bigger than any course most of the riders had ever seen. The order of go was Don Sachey and Plain Sailing; Denny Emerson and Victor Dakin; Bruce Davidson and Irish Cap, and Mike Plumb and Good Mixture. Plain Sailing was no stranger to Burghley having competed there in 1966 at the first World Championships with Rosemary Kopanski. With his experience, I felt he would be sure to get around, and Don could then pass on valuable information to his teammates. Unfortunately, Plain Sailing had a fall on the course, which put the pressure on the other three. Now, instead of going for personal success, the riders had to concentrate on what was best for the team, and they all rose to the occasion. All three horses went clear with Mike posting one of the fastest times of the day, all of which led to the US being in the lead going into the final show-jumping phase. Mark Phillips and H.M. The Queen's Columbus had gone into the lead individually with the fastest time, but unfortunately, Columbus had injured himself at the end of the course and was withdrawn the next day, a true heartbreaker for Mark. That left Bruce in the lead with Mike just 24/100 of a point behind. Beth Perkins had gone clear on Furtive, but Caroline Treviranus and Cajun had fallen resulting in a broken collar-bone for Caroline.

All the American horses passed the veterinary inspection thanks to the care given by all the ground staff of the US team overnight. There was no doubt that the pressure on Bruce in the show jumping was enormous. Young Beth Perkins, broken foot and all, jumped herself and Furtive into sixth place overall. Mike jumped clear with Good Mixture to finish on 71.93. Just one second over the time would drop Bruce to second place. But he and Irish Cap kept it all together and jumped clear, and his score of 71.67 clinched not only the first individual world championship gold medal for the US but also the team gold medal. I had achieved one of my ambitions. I had coached a gold medal team in world-class competition. Now I wanted to add the Olympic team gold medal.

After the Americans had won, Richard Meade came and congratulated me. "Richard," I said, "I don't know if you have a good memory, but I want you to know I always keep my promises." I am sure he knew to what I referred.

Neil Ayer, generous as ever, threw a grand party to celebrate our victory although I am not sure how many of us could remember much about it the next day!

MARY ANNE, MARCUS AURELIUS, AND LEDYARD '75!

Sometimes it seems like Marcus Aurelius and Mary Anne Tauskey appeared from nowhere and took the eventing world completely unawares. Mary Anne was an American, but she and her family had been living in England for a while, and it was there she had "found" eventing. She also found the little horse that I came to call "The Bionic Pony." He was only 15.1, but he didn't know it. He had done a couple of novice (Preliminary) competitions with a young girl in England and was too strong for her, so she had decided to sell him. Mary Anne liked what she saw and when she sat on him she liked him even more. She and her new horse moved into Wylie with Lord and Lady Hugh Russell who helped her do some serious training there. Mary Anne became a working student and to make ends meet she worked as a waitress at the Old Forge Inn. In fact, she was there when the team arrived for their onslaught on the World Championships at Burghley, and we stayed at the Inn with Mary Anne waiting on us. She did not miss any opportunity to watch the training sessions and was there for every single one.

Marcus and Mary Anne did a few events in England, finishing up with the three-day event at Wylie. Then they headed for the States and in an amazingly short time were entered in "Ledyard '75" with Mary Anne applying for consideration for the short list. Quite bold of her to say she had done her first event just one year before. The Bionic Pony zipped around Neil's course and finished in sixth place forcing us to take notice. Mary Anne and Marcus Aurelius had just bought themselves a place on the shortlist for the Pan Ams in Mexico later that summer.

"Ledyard '75" almost didn't happen. To put on an event of this magnitude, it takes about 300 volunteers and several hundreds of thousands of dollars. The financing comes through sponsorships and private money. Shipping in foreign horses and riders is very expensive but in this situation, it was the only way to entice good riders from other countries to come to Ledyard. The event organizers chartered a plane from Europe to bring several European riders over, and I have to say I thought our good friends the Brits took full advantage of the situation. They put on that plane not only the riders and horses but their families, grandmas, aunts, uncles, and every piece of equipment they could imagine. I think the only thing they forgot was the kitchen sink. Neil and his wife Helen, with their usual kindness and generosity, looked after everybody but in addition to the incredible amount of work that goes into such a production, the financial aspect was a tough challenge. Without a title sponsor such as Lexington, Kentucky has in Rolex, organizers constantly struggled to make ends meet.

Concerned about financing, Neil was forced to go to the USCTA membership and ask for donations to support the event. The USCTA had approximately 3,000 members at the time and two-thirds of those were juniors leaving just 1,000 adults to bear the brunt. Neil needed to raise $60,000 and asked if each of the 1,000 adult members could donate $50 or so. "Some members will want to help out in the hundreds of dollars. Others will not be able to participate to this extent—but the average should work out at something just over $50—in retrospect, not an enormous amount to help ensure the future of a sport all of us are so heavily involved in." Such was Neil's personality that the membership responded and "Ledyard '75" was a reality. It was given a big boost by the presence of H.R.H. Princess Anne and her then husband Mark Phillips who both competed. Many of today's riders (including Karen O'Connor) credit Ledyard as the inspiration for becoming eventers themselves.

Bruce Davidson was teamed up with Golden Griffin at Ledyard '75, and together they put up a brilliant performance to win the competition relegating the winner of Ledyard '73, Sue Hatherly, and Harley, into second place. Bruce was third with Royal Core and Tad Coffin, still riding as a junior, was fourth with Bally Cor. Tad won the Junior Preliminary Championship that was run at Ledyard the same weekend. Michael Tucker, now well known as an FEI official course designer and a BBC commentator, placed fifth on Ben Wyvis with Marcus Aurelius and Mary Anne coming in sixth.

You may be wondering how the team came to own Roger Haller's horse, Golden Griffin. Earlier in the year, Roger had made the decision to take the horse to Badminton where he met with two very disappointing events. Golden Griffin performed very badly in the dressage phase putting himself way down at the bottom of the rankings and then was denied the chance to redeem himself on his strongest phase, the cross-country when the competition was canceled due to the appalling weather. They were able to complete the briefings and the dressage phase, but the grounds were a morass of mud and the potential of doing tremendous damage to Badminton's Park was so great that it was decided to abandon the event. Roger's father was heard to say that this had to be the most expensive dressage test ever!

Upon returning to the US Roger had to concentrate on his career in his family business and decided to sell Golden Griffin. Having worked with the horse I knew that there was a definite problem with his dressage, but I believed that with a concentrated effort it could be fixed. He was such a great cross-country horse that I felt it was worth asking Raymond Firestone (who had previously bought Plain Sailing) if he would consider buying Golden Griffin. Ray with his usual supportive attitude bought "Fred" and gave him to the team. Having committed myself to this extent I took on the task of riding the horse myself every day and often several times a day. His dressage improved so much that I considered entering him for Ledyard. As he had not gone cross-country at Badminton, I could keep him in work, and I galloped him myself to keep up his conditioning. I was so impressed with his progress that only a couple of weeks before Ledyard I called Bruce and offered him the ride. Bruce was understandably skeptical as he had never ridden him before, and he knew his reputation in the dressage arena. I assured Bruce that he would be very rideable in the dressage and that he was ready to go. Bruce came up a couple of days before, rode Fred a couple of times and the rest is history.

I felt very confident as we now began preparing for the Pan Am Games. I had a solid pool of horses and riders from which to pick a potential gold medal team. I wish I could have been as confident about what to expect in Mexico.

10

1975 Pan Am Games

The 1975 Pan American Games in Mexico were a real eye-opener regarding fair play. Used to the army tradition in Europe where rules and regulations were adhered to implicitly, it came as something of a shock to realize that we were pretty much dealing with borderline outlaws serving as Mexican Army organizers.

Much of it was due to the influence of former Mexican Army General Marilles. General Marilles had ridden on the Mexican Show Jumping Team in the 1948 Olympic Games in London and had won the individual gold medal. There was no doubt he was a good rider, but his personality was another thing entirely. He came from an era when violence and intimidation won the day, and he was nothing more than a thug. During his competitive days in Mexico, he would see a horse that he liked and ask how much the owner wanted. The owner would say that the horse was not for sale. Two days later an army truck would show up, and Marilles would quite simply take the horse. He believed that through his connections—he was related to the then president—he could escape any consequences of his actions. This belief failed him when a new president was elected. Not being smart enough to figure out that a new president might not overlook the behavior that his relative turned a blind eye to, he was finally jailed for several years for shooting the father of seven children in the back during a minor traffic altercation. The man died at the scene. The prison though was not quite the type of prison that you and I would normally envision. Marilles was pretty much under house arrest with servants taking care of his every need.

After years of incarceration, Marilles was freed and soon after he traveled to Paris where he was arrested carrying drugs. He was found hanged in his cell the following day, and no one knows if he took his own life.

MAÑANA

General Marilles' way of dealing with life was still very much in practice in the Mexican cavalry when we were there in 1975. The Pan Am Games were held in Mexico City with the army camp being the venue for many activities. The difficulties started almost immediately. Everything was *mañana*, which meant it never happened as it would always be tomorrow. There definitely was a plan to disrupt the American team, and it was impossible to find out when we could get access to the arenas to train, which meant that very little training was done at all. During the endurance test on the roads and tracks there was an army band playing. Every time an American would go out the band would set up in the middle of the track and start playing. Mary Anne Tauskey's Marcus Aurelius went berserk. The track at this point went between steep banks on either side. How Mary Anne ever got that horse up the hill and around the band I will never know, but it thoroughly rattled Marcus Aurelius and was totally unfair.

The worst one was when a fence judge jumped out and grabbed at Golden Griffin's bridle when he and Bruce Davidson were approaching on cross-country to take off over a fence. Apparently, Jim Day of Canada had been eliminated, and the officials sent word that he had to be stopped. Unfortunately, the horse they stopped was Golden Griffin. The official ran out, grabbed the reins and pulled.

The horse was committed to the jump and continued to take off, but his balance was off so badly he couldn't make it, and he and Bruce fell. Bruce was smart enough to get back on and jump the fence again and continued to the finish, but I believe that the manner of the fall set in motion a leg problem with the horse that resulted in his breakdown one month later.

Pip Graham from Canada was the Technical Delegate, and he had his hands full correcting all the errors on the score sheets. Bally Cor and Tad Coffin went clean and fast, but there were significant time penalties posted on their score on Roads and Tracks. Thank God for Pip who saw it and was strong enough to sort it all out.

Back in 1955, the Pan Am Games had also been held in Mexico and then-USET President Whitney Stone had been outraged by some very similar behavior exhibited by those in authority at the Games. He launched a protest against the very same kind of problem, unwarranted penalties added to the scores of US riders. Marilles was the president of the Jury of Appeals at those particular Games and as such had to deal with the protest. He walked into the meeting room, took out his handgun and put it on the table. "Anyone got anything to say here?" he said. But Whitney Stone would not give in to that kind of intimidation and said: "Yes, I do." The matter was resolved but that was the type of atmosphere that prevailed in Mexico during the Marilles era, and there was no doubt that not much had changed by 1975.

When all the controversy (at least for that day) was over, the correct scores were finally posted. Golden Griffin had only 15.2 time penalties in spite of the hullabaloo that went on while he was on course; Bally Cor had 28.8, and Beth and Furtive had 56.4. Little Marcus Aurelius, being the first out, had suffered the most from all the harassment and his score for the speed and endurance was 118.8. He and Mary Anne would again take the brunt of the storm as first out for the Americans in the show jumping phase.

A friend of mine was the chef d'equipe of the Guatemalan team. He told me that a rumor was circulating that the US horses were drugged. I thanked him for the information and went straight to the Ground Jury and requested samples be taken on all my horses—not just one sample but two, one for them and one for me. The samples were taken and tested. I never heard one more word.

On the final day of show jumping, they gave us absolutely no time to walk the course. We had to run around the jumps, and we were still in the ring when they started calling for the first horse. Of course, the first horse was Marcus Aurelius and while he was warmed up on the flat a little he had jumped no fences. The fences in the warm-up were left over from the show jumping competition. The oxer was around six feet or so. I asked Patrick Lynch who traveled with me everywhere to lower the fences for Mary Anne. He went to drop the rail and a man appeared with a gun and pointed it at him. "You are not allowed to touch that fence," he said. This whole time they were calling for Mary Anne to come into the ring and were threatening to disqualify her for not entering the ring in a timely manner. There was a young officer there, and I asked him to go and get someone in charge to help out. The ring steward started yelling that Mary Anne was eliminated, and I shouted at this guy and asked who was in charge. "Major Daza," he replied. I yelled, "Get the major in here now!"

I told Patrick to lower the fence, and the lieutenant got in front of him. I saw Patrick's hands come up and go for the man's throat. I yelled to Patrick not to touch him as I knew he was going to strangle the guy, and it was more than likely that the soldier would shoot.

Mary Anne was standing there watching all this take place, and I just said, "Do not worry darling, we will fix this, don't get upset." As tough and dragon-like as I was at home, I was the rider's best friend in competition and did everything possible to support them and make sure they were fully prepared for the test.

Finally, a man came and lowered the rails and Mary Anne got to warm up. Marcus Aurelius gave it his all and got away with just two rails down, a score matched by Bally Cor. Golden Griffin, who I believe was feeling the effects of his tumultuous round the day before, had 20 penalties, as did Furtive. Nevertheless, they did what was needed, and we secured the gold medal for the Team and of course Tad won the individual gold on Bally Cor with Bruce and Golden Griffin taking the silver. Interestingly, the Mexicans had great show jumping horses as all three of their riders jumped clear to take the team bronze medal behind Canada, who took the silver. Captain David Barcena of Mexico and Abordage won the individual bronze. Beth and Furtive finished fifth, and Mary Anne and Marcus Aurelius were seventh.

TROPHIES AT LARGE

Our troubles with the Mexican Army organizers were not yet over. We had now been on site for over two weeks, as our experience from the 1968 Mexico Olympics told me that we needed that amount of time for the horses to acclimatize to the altitude. For the entire time prior to and during the championships the trophies had been on display in the officers' mess where we all ate our meals.

Jack Burton was a VP of the USET at that time and was chef de mission for the U.S teams. At the presentation, I asked him to look into how we would get the trophies home as they were quite big and I wondered if they came apart for shipping.

I had had two weeks of nonstop 24-hour days dealing with the Mexicans and was burned out and needed some breathing space. I left right after the presentations and went to nearby Silvertown to let down a little. I returned the following day and had a message from Jack. He asked if I was okay and had rested up a bit and then went on to say, "You know those trophies, well they have gone back to the Army, they do not want to give them to us." I told Jack, "You are a military man and can speak the language of these guys. Tell them to put them where the sun doesn't shine and rotate!" We never got the trophies!

The Guatemalan chef told me later that they had won some trophies which they had been given only to have them confiscated at the border of Mexico when they left. It spoke volumes as to how the Mexicans ran equestrian sports at that time. It all came from the influence of General Marilles who had competed in his younger days at Madison Square Garden and in Europe and had done things that were despicable and which would not have been tolerated today.

The 1975 Pan Am Games in Mexico were the hardest of all the competitions in my entire career, and I thank God for that! I am delighted to say that things are much different today, and the US has a very good relationship with the Mexican Federation. They have some fine riders, some of whom train here in the US. In fact, today the USEA is working with the Mexican Federation to develop a program to teach and train Mexican instructors for USEA certification.

11

THE ROAD TO MONTREAL

The Olympic year always follows the Pan Ams and our results in Mexico in 1975 should have left us in a strong position looking forward to Montreal. However, not only had Golden Griffin come up lame following the outrageous incident on the Pan Am cross-country course but Victor Dakin and Good Mixture were recovering from injuries sustained after the Burghley World Championships. In 1975, Irish Cap had come down with a lung infection which had almost cost him his life and Beth Perkins' Furtive had been retired to Huntington Farm in Vermont after helping win the Pan Am gold medal. Unfortunately, he did not get to enjoy his retirement as he broke his leg and was put down in March of 1976. Beth and Furtive had been in training with me since before the 1974 World Championships, and I was saddened to hear of the loss of such a great horse.

There were three selection trials planned for the spring: Ship's Quarters in Maryland, Middletown in Delaware and Blue Ridge in Virginia. From the long list of riders who had applied to be candidates for the Team a short list would be selected based on the results of these three competitions. The shortlisted riders would train with me at Team Headquarters, and the team of four plus one reserve rider would be picked for the Games which were to be held July 22 to 25 at Bromont in Quebec.

Neil Ayer, President of the USCTA at that time, summed up our chances in an article in the then *USCTA News* of May 1976:

"We have only six horses that have competed as many times as twice in an International Three-Day Event. They are Good Mixture (belonging to the USET and 2nd at Burghley), Irish Cap (belonging to Bruce Davidson, 1st at Burghley and 3rd at Badminton in 1974), Golden Griffin (USET, 1st at Ledyard, and 2nd at the Pan Am Games in '75), Bally Cor (USET 4th at Ledyard and 1st in Mexico in '75) Marcus Aurelius (Mary Anne Tauskey, 6th at Ledyard and 7th at the Pan Am Games in '75), and Cajun (ridden both at Ledyard and at Burghley by Caroline Treviranus). Of these six, Irish Cap and Good Mixture are back in work after long layoffs due to sickness and injury and Golden Griffin will be missing at least the first of the Olympic Selection Trials because he has not yet sufficiently recovered from injuries sustained in Mexico. Only time will tell whether or not Cappy and Mixture are up to the fast work that will be required of them and Golden Griffin would, at this juncture, have to be classified as a questionable starter. Of the other campaigners that have made it to the top Denny Emerson's Victor Dakin (Team Gold medal, Burghley, 14th individually) has been out of competition since 1974 but is now back in training and Tad Zimmerman's Fine Tune (7th Ledyard with the fastest cross-country time) and Mike Plumb's Carillon have been working for several months with the Olympic Selection Trials in view.

"With a shortage of experienced horses (and particularly with three or four of them with unsoundness in their past) Coach Jack Le Goff has been devoting much time in bringing along such combinations as Kevin Freeman on his young Egan Way, Beth Perkins on Tyson, The Sheik, and Tor, Jimmy Wofford on Touch and Go, Mike Plumb on Better and Better, Tad Coffin on Road to Ko-Ro-Ba and The Swamp Fox, and Caroline Treviranus on Comic Relief. Few of these horses have much three-day experience at the higher levels behind them but with the lack of depth we have it only makes sense to try to bring them along to the point where one or more of them can fill in as a substitute at the last minute. We should also remember that over thirty candidates have declared themselves and will be competing at the three Selection Trials. It wouldn't be a bit surprising to see one of them come to the fore, the way Mary Anne Tauskey and Marcus Aurelius did last year, right out of nowhere so to speak, and end up on the short list for Montreal. The proving ground will be Ships Quarters, Middletown, and Blue Ridge. So very much will depend on how the experienced horses hold up and how the inexperienced horses progress at the three trials.

"What are our chances for a gold medal? Perhaps our greatest single asset is our coach Jack Le Goff. His horses and his riders will be as well trained and as well prepared as time and past experience and soundness will permit. Jack Le Goff is the most respected three-day coach in the world today. He can be expected to, and will produce a number of minor miracles but he can't be expected to accomplish the impossible. What it all boils down to is that if our good horses stay sound we have as good a chance as we have ever had to win a gold."

While I very much appreciated Neil's generous remarks, I did feel that to succeed we would be pulling off the impossible and I knew that the next few months would be very much uphill. While our young riders Tad, Mary Anne, and Beth had produced career-best rides in Mexico at the Pan Ams, we had to face the fact that the Olympic Games are a challenge unto themselves and the pressure is at a level not experienced anywhere else. In those circumstances, it is always advisable whenever possible to have experienced, well-seasoned horses and riders who have "been there and done that."

NATURAL SELECTION
Many countries, including Britain, use a natural selection process whereby riders are left to their own devices regarding their day-to-day training. The selectors look at the results of specific events

and then select the consistently successful ones for a short training session before the big competition. My aim was always to prepare as many riders as possible to develop a wider and deeper pool of talent. That was what my four-year plan was all about, identifying those riders with potential and then providing consistent and ongoing training. I could only take four riders at a time into intensive training, but to get down to those four, I would have looked at and worked with hundreds. I was always looking for that extra something. Many competent riders are relatively successful but lack that extra something that makes the international star. That something is the competitive spirit, and it is born into a rider. If it is not there, no one can put it there. Having those riders work with me consistently over a nine-month period each year enabled me to see how the riders would stand up to pressure because I put pressure on them and in no uncertain terms. If they couldn't survive pressure from me what would happen when they went out in front of a panel of international judges and thousands of spectators.

The pressure came from my being very demanding in all aspects of competition and phases of training. I was never completely satisfied. I made them study the rule book. I insisted on them being on time for lessons and properly dressed, and their horses properly turned out. They had to stay in good physical condition, and I weighed the riders regularly. Strict self-discipline was expected and to ensure the younger riders did not get swelled heads I used to tell them, "There is only one movie star around here, and it happens to be me!" I was joking, but they were smart and got my point.

Each rider was different and had to be handled accordingly. Tad Coffin was a very talented rider, but he did not always believe how good he was so I looked for opportunities during a competition to give him confidence.

At the beginning of his career, Bruce Davidson was trying too hard to ride correctly. He would get caught at the beginning of the cross-country course because he was not riding aggressively and would sometimes have a stop at an easy fence. My solution was to get him furious at me (something I found very easy to do) right before he started on course. He would then go out of the start box ready to take on the world! All it means is knowing each rider and communicating with him or her accordingly.

But, while the riders often didn't like the way I dealt with them on a daily basis I know they knew that I was the one person they could rely on in all things at the competition. It was my role to relieve them of all outside distractions so they could concentrate solely on the job at hand. Some have said I was omnipresent, and that is an excellent compliment for it means that I didn't miss anything; I was there for them in all things. I considered that essential to do my job properly, and it would be no different in Montreal.

In the end, the team was picked on performance; not necessarily on objectivity alone because subjectivity has to play a large part if the goal is to send the team most likely to bring home the gold medal. The selection process is part of the preparation process, and it is progressive. My approach was not to eliminate horses and riders but to prepare as many as I could so that there was a wide choice available when the time came. Part of the preparation included educating the riders on how to handle disappointment. The hardest part about being the coach was having to tell a rider that he or she will not be on the team, and that happened in Montreal.

As it turned out, and thanks to careful conditioning, we were lucky to have Irish Cap, Good Mixture, Victor Dakin, and Golden Griffin sound and available for shipping. We took five riders and seven horses to Bromont: Mike Plumb with Good Mixture and Better and Better, Bruce Davidson with Irish Cap and Golden Griffin, Tad Coffin with Bally Cor, Denny Emerson with Victor Dakin, and Mary Anne Tauskey with Marcus Aurelius.

MONTREAL OLYMPICS

Montreal, as a consequence of Munich, involved tremendous security procedures, which were understandable, but nevertheless difficult to handle. The schedule worked very well for us. First, we were allowed to walk the course. Then came the presentation of all the horses for inspection with the declaration of the team set for the next morning. Walking the course, I found it to be fairly soft in terms of difficulty. The fences were all up to height, but there was not the level of technicality that we had started to see in cross-country course design in the seventies. A few of the jumps posed some legitimate questions but overall for the Olympics, it was not in keeping with the evolution of courses at that time. The statistics would later show that it proved a very valid level of competition and some of that might have had more to do with the rigorous roads and tracks, which were very hilly and likely contributed to some tired horses out on Phase D.

Having seen the course, I sat down with Mike to talk about which horse would be best suited to be on the team. Good Mixture had all the experience and was a fabulous cross-country horse, but he was older and though perfectly sound we couldn't completely disregard the fact that he had been injured the previous year. Better and Better while young and inexperienced was totally sound and was a much better mover than Good Mixture. If the cross-country course was not going to be the deciding factor in the competition, we would have to rely on some strong dressage performances. I asked Mike what he thought and told him it was up to him to choose. He felt that Better and Better would be the best choice as with Mixture's history of leg problems he wouldn't be suited to the hilly terrain, nor the sandy track of the steeplechase. With Better and Better being much the better dressage horse (he was originally started by Carol Lavell, who went on to win the 1992 Olympic bronze medal in dressage on Gifted) Mike chose to ride him for the team. Today, Better and Better would not be qualified for this level of competition as I don't think he had yet done an Advanced three-day event, but back in 1976, he was!

It was originally planned to have Denny Emerson and Victor Dakin ride on the team with Bruce, Mike, and Tad, but after the last gallop I checked all the horses' legs, and it was evident to me that Victor Dakin was showing signs of pending leg trouble. I knew that Denny would be bitterly disappointed, but I had to ask myself what was the point of sending a horse to the Olympics if there is a chance that he will not finish on the last day. Mary Anne Tauskey and Marcus Aurelius were named to the team instead. Denny was unprepared for that. He was extremely upset and understandably just wanted to go home. I asked him to stay and help his teammates in the competition, which he did, and I think he was very glad that he did. He had never thought of the possibility of not making the team so he had not thought out how he would react if and when the time came. I believe all riders should be prepared for the possibility of disappointment as that can be devastating after everything they have invested in the effort to make a team.

Mary Anne and her bionic pony were the first to go in dressage. Mary Anne at 5 feet 2 inches and Marcus Aurelius at 15.1 were the "David" going up against "Goliath," and the crowd took them to their hearts. Unfortunately, they cheered so loudly as she entered the ring Marcus got too fired up, and she had all she could do to keep the lid on him. Riding with great sympathy, she got him through it, but the test scored a 97.09. Tad and Bally Cor arrived in the ring to much the same welcome, but the mare was able to hold it together to go into second place on 64.59 behind West Germany's Otto Ammerman on the super stallion Volturno. Bally Cor was a poor mover but was very obedient. Tad did a great job and rode a very precise and accurate test without one single mistake. Quite an achievement in Olympic competition!

Our two riders had put the team into first place just 5.82 penalties ahead of the West Germans. Britain's Hugh Thomas (who was to go on to become the director of the Badminton Horse Trials) was in third place on Playamar. H.R.H. Princess Anne, riding Goodwill, was, of course, the big media attraction of the Games. She was under more pressure than any other rider there and the non-equestrian paparazzi did not let up on her. She deserved a great deal of credit for keeping a very cool head and not allowing the unrelenting attention to affect her.

The next day Madrigal, ridden by another West German, Karl Schultz, took the lead on 46.25. Bruce and Irish Cap excelled and were rewarded with second place on 54.16. The young and relatively green Better and Better scored well on 66.25, which put the United States in the lead over West Germany by 1.66 penalties.

Speed and endurance day proved daunting for many. Thunder and lightning ushered in the day and though it cleared some-what, dark clouds and intermittent rain made the going soggy and energy sapping.

Otto Ammerman missed the final flags on steeplechase and incurred numerous time penalties for having to ride Volturno back to cor-rect the mistake. He was then eliminated because of "unauthorized assistance" as it was deemed that the very noisy crowd had pointed his mistake out to him—heartbreaking for such a talented horse with such huge potential.

Marcus Aurelius was first out on course for the United States and Mary Anne had been told to go steadily and conservatively. She incurred two refusals but came home with lots of information to pass on to her teammates. Theirs was the best round of any of the previous eight horses.

Princess Anne and Goodwill were going well until fence 19 when the horse tipped over. Princess Anne was knocked unconscious for a split second but got back on and completed the next seventeen fences on the course. Today that would not be permitted, but it tes-tified to her amazing tenacity and pluck.

The first third of the starting order produced only three clear rounds: two for Australia by riders Denis Pigott and Mervyn Bennet and one for France, rider Jean-Yves Touzaint.

The second third included Tad and Bally Cor who posted the fastest clear of the day. Karl Schultz and Madrigal also jumped clear. This group fared a little better and produced eight clear rounds in total, with Herbert Blocker being the hero of the day when he lost his stirrup leather at Fence 11 and rode the rest of the course without stirrups at all.

The last 16 could only come up with four clear rounds, and fortunately for the United States, Mike Plumb and Better and Better were among them. Lucinda Prior-Palmer (now Green) put in a brilliant round on her Be Fair who had won her Badminton in 1973 and the 1975 European championships in Luhmuhlen. Sadly, for Be Fair, he tore an Achilles tendon on his way to the finish and had to be withdrawn. Earlier in the day, Hugh Thomas had suffered a fall during his round and Playamar had pulled up lame, which, while we didn't know it at the time, put the British team out of contention.

Bruce and Irish Cap were going beautifully until the water jump when Cappy had his first fall ever in competition. Bruce was quickly back in the saddle and finished the course, and even with the fall, his round put the US into the lead by 73 points. Karl Schultz held the lead individually with Tad in second and Mike Plumb in third.

All of our horses were tired and a little stiff but Marty Simensen, the team veterinarian, pronounced them sound and well. It was the first time in the six Olympic Games I had been involved with that I had four hale and hearty horses going into the final day, and I knew that the decision to put the younger horses on the team had been the right one. Out of 12 teams of some 49 competitors from 13 countries, seven teams for a total of 30 riders completed the course. Almost 25 percent of the competitors were either eliminated or retired on course. Sixty-one percent of the entry completed the entire competition, which was a rather low percentage for that caliber of competition.

We were terribly sad for the British Team who had fallen out of contention with two lame horses, but with their true sportsmanlike spirit they rose above their disappointment, and all congratulated the Americans.

The show jumping the next day did nothing to change the standings for the teams and the gold went to the United States on 441.0, the silver to West Germany on 584.60 and the bronze to Australia with 599.54.

Though the show jumping didn't affect the team standings, it had a significant impact on the individual medals. Bally Cor jumped a beautiful clear round for Tad, but Better and Better put a foot in the water for five penalties. Madrigal and Karl Schultz tried to keep their first place, but it wasn't to be. The overnight leader of both the first and second days pulled two rails dropping to the bronze medal position and elevating Tad to gold and Mike to silver. Britain's Richard Meade rode Jacob Jones into fourth place and H.R.H. Princess Anne, none the worse for her crashing fall the previous day, rode a polished round to finish 24th with just 3.25 time penalties.

And so, I had finally achieved my Olympic dream: to coach a gold medal team. I was well pleased. But when I went back home to Hamilton, I was really at a loss. I had finally reached my goal, and I didn't know where to go from there. I shared my thinking with Madeleine, who always supported me, in the good and challenging times. However, as in most cases when questions are troubling me, I go fishing. So, I took my boat and went out on the ocean, and when I came back, I had an answer. I admitted the fact that although I had reached my goal, it would probably be at least an equal challenge to keep the team at the top of international competition. It was sufficient to motivate me for the next years to come.

12

MIGHT TANGO

When I lived in Europe, I always owned at least one horse, somehow, some way. After Montreal, I badly needed more horses for the team and decided I was going to look around for a horse to buy. I would put the horse in my wife Madeleine's name and have her loan him to the team. It was a big sacrifice for me as we had little spare money at the time but I wanted to do it.

I knew that one of Bruce's friends, Mr. Tindall, frequently went out West and brought back a load of horses from off the racetracks to resell. I told him of my plan to look for a horse, and he said there was one not too far away that looked pretty good to him. The lady that owned him was married to a vet and had bought the horse to train and sell on.

I asked Bruce to go with me. It was the week of the Radnor Three-Day Event and by the time we got through with the event and over to see the horse it was getting dark. I liked the look of him and wanted to see him under saddle. I asked Bruce to get on and ride him, and he walked, trotted, and cantered him around. There was a chute with some rails set up, and he went through that easily. I asked the owner how much she wanted for the horse. It is always best to ask the price straight away; you don't want the owner to see how much you like the horse and put the price up, nor do you want to waste your time or theirs if there is no way you would ever be able to pay a high price. The owner was asking $5,000. She would make a bit of money because she had only had the horse a couple of weeks and had not paid anywhere near that. I asked if she would give me her word that the horse was not on any drugs that would mask any lameness. She did, and I told her the horse was sold. "You're not going to vet him?" she asked in surprise. I told her no, that it was almost dark, and he had just jumped through the chute, so I knew his eyes were fine. He was not drugged, and he performed well, so I bought him there and then. She was aghast, but I have bought horses like that all my life. The other horse I bought the same way was Blue Stone who would take Mike Plumb to his seventh Olympic Games in Los Angeles.

The following morning, I sent Patrick Lynch with the van and a check for $5,000. Marty Simensen was the team vet at that time, and I said to him, "Marty, I want you to vet this horse because I want to loan him to the team and I want to make sure the team is protected."

Marty was astounded that I had not had the horse vetted before I handed over the check, and duly gave him a thorough examination. "You sure saved yourself a lot of money, Jack," he said. "This horse is perfectly sound and healthy." I knew it really; he had done nothing except not race very well, and that not for very long, and probably jumped his first jump the night before so I knew he did not have a lot of mileage on him.

People are very strange, and that was made clear to me after I loaned Might Tango to the Team. It was reported to me that people said because Madeleine and I owned the horse it would be favored when it came to team selection and put on the team over other horses. That disturbed and amazed me because that is not the way I work and never would be. If anything I would have been more critical of a horse owned by myself or my family. The paperwork was underway but not signed and sealed and when I realized what was being said I stopped the loan process immediately. I called Bruce in and asked him if he remembered the horse. He did. "Well, Bruce," I said, "For personal reasons I am not going to loan him to the team and I think he is a good horse with a lot of potential and I will sell him to you for exactly what I paid for him on the condition that you will never sell him for a profit." After putting in a few months of work on the horse, I could have sold him for quite a bit more than that, and I was out of pocket on the deal. Bruce bought him and rode him into the record books.

THE 1978 WORLD CHAMPIONSHIPS

Several selection trials for the World Championships were held through the first half of 1978 beginning with Middleburg, Ships Quarters, and Blue Ridge in the spring running through Ledyard in July and culminating at Chesterland in Pennsylvania. Chesterland held a two-day event, which meant we ran dressage and show jumping on the first day and endurance on the second. This format allowed the horses to rest after the cross-country phase as they would not be asked to jump again and any minor injuries would not be stressed and given every chance to heal. At the end of the competition, I announced the short list for Lexington: Tad Coffin, Bruce Davidson, Mike Plumb, Mary Anne Tauskey, Torrance Watkins, and Jim Wofford. From the six I would choose the four team members, and the remaining two would ride as individuals. I always tried to do this at the last possible minute as experience had proven to me that horses have a way to go wrong at a crucial time. I also had to choose the riders who would take up the additional individual slots that we were entitled to as the host country of the championships. Those riders were Mary Hazzard, Ralph Hill, Mike Huber, Story Jenks, Desiree Smith, and Caroline Treviranus. I had an additional "on call" list in case any of the riders on the first two lists fell out of the running. These were Rebecca Coffin, Lornie Forbes, Tom Glascock, and Karen

Reuter Sachey. Sadly, Derek di Grazia's Thriller II had been injured at Ledyard and was not available for selection. The work now began.

Bruce was one of those in the enviable position of having two horses in contention, the current world champion Irish Cap and Might Tango, even though I wasn't seriously thinking about Tango as he was very young and wouldn't be ready for Lexington. Mike had Laurenson and Better and Better who were both in top shape. Mike, however, was not, having torn his gracillis muscle at Ledyard and we were keeping a close eye on his "soundness." Jim Wofford had the brilliant Carawich in top form for us also. I have to say one thing about Carawich as I rode him on many occasions. Once you got on him, it was almost impossible to get off. He was without a doubt one of the best horses I have ever had the privilege to ride, a real Rolls Royce of a horse.

Tad had the gallant mare Bally Cor, the darling of the eventing world at that time, and Mary Anne Tauskey had Marcus Aurelius. The newcomer to the team, Torrance Watkins, was lucky enough to have two horses to choose from: Red's Door and Severo. Now the goal would be to keep everyone, both horses, and riders, sound, healthy and fit to compete until September.

There was much to be done on many fronts. When Bruce Davidson won the 1974 World Championships, the US was asked to host the 1978 championships. (Incidentally, unlike today, in the 1970s the individual performance rather than the team performance is what determined the host country of the next championships.) The national federation, the American Horse Shows Association (forerunner of the USEF—the United States Equestrian Federation) set to work to find a site that could support such an immense undertaking. Dr. James B. Holloway and Mrs. Edith Conyers, backed by Kentucky's governor, Julian E. Carroll, put in the Lexington, Kentucky bid. Once that was accepted there was lots of excitement, not only about the actual World Championship competition, but also about the opening of the Kentucky Horse Park, which was to coincide with the championships.

Roger Haller was selected to design the course at Kentucky along with course-builder Richard Newton, and we knew it would not be an easy course. I also knew that I would have to present the horses at their peak of fitness to face this challenge, especially as the weather in Kentucky in September would likely still be quite warm. What I, and others, didn't anticipate was the extreme heat and humidity that we would face that week and the awful toll it would take on the horses, especially the older ones.

STEPPING ON THEIR BEARDS

Bally Cor was now 13, and Irish Cap was showing signs of his age. Bruce competed him very lightly and had concentrated on the trials at Ledyard. He won that in high style and looked like he could defend his title if all went well. I had made a plea for more young horses earlier in the year to replace those who are "stepping on their beards." It always takes a while to produce a truly seasoned horse, especially a contender for the Olympics and World Championships, so I was thinking more about horses for the future rather than for 1978. At Ledyard, I had been very impressed with Might Tango's progress and knew he would be a serious international prospect in a couple of years. I had given the riders strict instructions to go easy on the cross-country course and not go for speed as I did not want the World Championships to be lost before we ever got to Kentucky. As it was, Might Tango came out at the final trials at Chesterland and performed the winning dressage test, jumped out of his skin across country making it look like a schooling course and impressed the selectors to no end. Even with this performance, it was Irish Cap who was named as Bruce's first horse.

The 12 riders named to the Kentucky short list went into serious training at Chesterland. As the preparation intensified, I became more concerned regarding Irish Cap's soundness. In the morning the horses were jogged before work and Cappy was getting worse behind as the days passed. I talked to Bruce about it, but he had such love (and well deserved) for that horse that he could not accept the reality of Cappy being lame. At the end of the day, I made the decision to take Tango who, although very young, was sound, as I feared Cappy many not pass the first horse inspection. Few riders, in my opinion, would be horsemen enough to take as young and inexperienced a horse as Might Tango to such a competition, but Bruce was without a doubt one of those few.

Immediately upon arriving in Kentucky, I knew we could potentially be in big trouble. The temperatures were up around 90 degrees and the humidity was hovering near 90 percent. It was like being under a hot wet blanket. The horses just stood dripping and listless in their stalls. Fortunately, the barns at the Kentucky Horse Park were excellent with large permanent box stalls, which allowed the horses the ability to move around and lie down with ease. There was also a good amount of electrical outlets so that fans could be hung in the stalls to keep the horses as comfortable as possible. Most importantly, there was easy access to a plentiful water supply, and we were going to need that more than anything else, except ice!

With his horses sidelined, Denny Emerson acted as my assistant coach and his opinion was that given the right weather conditions, the Horse Park was equal to Badminton and Burghley as one of the foremost event sites in the world; a position to which the park holds an even greater claim today. Denny, also concerned about the conditions, wrote in the USCTA News at the time that "the impression upon stepping off the airplane was intense, humid, palpable heat."

To counter this, we had the horses out at dawn for their workouts before the temperatures soared again. The footing on the racetrack at the Horse Park at that time of the summer was very hard and twice we shipped the horses to Masterson's Park to gallop where the footing was more forgiving.

I had seen just about every international cross-country course in existence over the previous 25 years and after the first course walk in Kentucky, my impression was that it was the biggest I had ever seen. Almost every fence was maximum height. A long Phase A, a two-and-a-half-mile steeplechase on undulating ground at 690 meters per minute, and a very long Phase C followed by such a big cross-country course worried me no end. I did not want the riders to know, but my stomach was churning at what this would do to the horses given the heat and humidity. I had made some unpopular statements in the past about lessening the severity of the three-day event, particularly shortening, or even eliminating, Phase C, and everything in my lifetime of experience was telling me that we could be facing a potential disaster in Kentucky. The British team vet, Peter Scott Dunn, was worried too feeling that what was acceptable in cool climates was very inappropriate under these conditions. The Ground Jury relented slightly and reduced the distance on Phase C by two kilometers, but that was all. The cross-country course was 7,695 meters long (4.7 miles) with an optimum speed of 570 meters per minute, with 33 obstacles requiring 39 jumping efforts.

Speed and endurance day dawned cooler than previous days and the horses that went out early certainly benefited, but that didn't last long, and gradually the heat was turned on. Denny was out on the steeplechase course and reported that some of the riders were coming in up to as much as 30 seconds under the time, suicidal in that heat. Might Tango was one of the early horses out and enjoyed cooler temperatures for the steeplechase. It was another story on the cross-country, and when he came in after jumping clear around a course that would eliminate 36 percent of the starters, Might Tango was in considerable distress with a temperature hovering at 108 degrees. I had never seen a horse reach that temperature and survive. I do believe that most veterinarians would say the same thing. Usually, horses come into the vet box at the end of cross-country with temperatures around 104 to 105 degrees which quickly drop to 101 to 102 degrees when proper cooling techniques are applied. Thanks to the brilliance of Dr. Marty Simensen and quick action by everyone involved this brave and heroic young horse was saved from a life-threatening situation. After working through one of the most agonizing situations I have seen, I immediately ran over to tell Denny to warn the riders to slow it down on steeplechase and try to save as much horse as they could for what was to come.

Out of 41 starters, only 26 finished cross-country, and none made it inside the time. Neil Ayer, then president of the USCTA, stated in the *USCTA News* of November/December, 1978: "Collected for these World Championships was the most talented and experienced field of horses and riders ever assembled for an international Three-Day Event. Olympic gold medalists Richard Meade and Tad Coffin, two-time European Champion and three-time Badminton winner Lucinda Prior-Palmer (now Green), many times leading US rider, Olympic and World silver medalist and Ledyard winner, Mike Plumb, Badminton winner Jane Holderness-Roddam with Warrior, Burghley winner Carawich with Jimmy Wofford, Chris Collins, Bruce Davidson, John Watson, Volturno, Sumatra; they were all there. Yet of the 41 that actually started on Phase D, 27 either never finished the course or had one or more falls that put them out of the running—this in spite of the fact that Roger Haller who designed the course did so . with every intention and hope that the boldest and most experienced horses and riders would finish at or near the top, the less seasoned and less talented toward the bottom, and those not ready for the test spun out somewhere along the line.

"For the first time in this country thousands (perhaps as many as a quarter of a million) spectators came to see what the sport of combined training was all about...they saw the sport take the biggest step backward since the step backward it took in 1964 at the Rome Olympics. Had it been a cool clear autumn day quite obviously many more horses would have crossed the finish line. Simply lobbing half a mile off of Phase B, reducing the speed on Phase D by 50 meters per minute, (things the Ground Jury could easily have done at the last minute without materially affecting the competition) would have made an enormous difference in the results."

In my book, every fence was a "genius" fence, but 33 genius fences do not produce a legitimately good course. After a big steeplechase, even the very good and experienced horses were suffering on the cross-country as there were few to no "breathers" on the course, and the word from a lot of knowledgeable people was that it was all too big. But from the public's point of view they sure got their money's worth. If today's rules had been in effect, where the first horse fall causes elimination, the show jumping day would have been a very quick affair because so few got around with less than that! Had steps been taken to modify the course in light of the extreme and hostile weather conditions, we would have seen a much better competition, one that would have boosted the sport not left us writhing uncomfortably trying to find ways to undo the public's perception of eventing. Today we call it damage control.

But, back to the championships! The course did throw up some real hopes for the future. The 18-year-old Mike Huber on the tough little six-year-old mare Gold Chip stormed around to finish even though they were one of those to fall at the infamous "Serpent" fence. They then took down just two rails in show jumping to finish 13th. Torrance Watkins and Red's Door had a similar fate with a few more time faults, and two show jumping rails to finish 15th. Mary Hazzard who had taken note of the toll that the course was having on the horses, cantered her Cavalistic around and finished clear but with many time penalties. Interestingly the horse jumped a clear show jumping round, and Mary finished 20th on possibly the freshest horse. But the real class performance came from Ralph Hill on Sergeant Gilbert who jumped clear with just 14.8 time penalties and who stood second to Bruce going into show jumping. Unfortunately, six rails dropped him to fourth, but it was a supreme effort by both horse and rider. Little Marcus Aurelius and Mary Anne suffered the indignity of a refusal, one of the very, very few the little horse ever had. She finished in 12th on a 169.4.

Out of the 12 riders, we had eight complete the course and only the gold medalists, Bruce and Might Tango, ended the competition in the double digits. Even with 20 penalties added in the show jumping Bruce ended on 93.4, and it was a testament to the care and hard work of the whole team that Might Tango was even able to jump the next day. The silver medal went to Ireland's John Watson on Cambridge Blue who finished on 120.6 penalties. The bronze medal went to Germany's Helmut Rethemeier and Ladalco on a final score of 122.8. Carawich came back from his fall at the Serpent the previous day and jumped clear with one time penalty to finish 10th. Tad Coffin and Bally Cor suffered two falls on cross-country and added 10 show jumping penalties to complete on a 274.8. Fortunately, Bruce, Jimmy, and Tad were able to keep the US in bronze medal position behind the Canadians and West Germany. Only three teams finished!

Before the competition, all the media, as well as all the top teams, were evaluating the chances of the United States, Great Britain, Germany, and France. No one was talking about the Canadians. I give them great credit for their performance. They played their cards very smartly and let the "big guys" fight it out. Their coaches did a super job of asking the riders and horses to simply do their job and not worry about the other guys. I do want to salute their excellent performance and the spirit that won them a well-deserved gold medal.

Two young men were at the championships in Kentucky in 1978. Mark Todd, an individual rider for New Zealand, rode a horse called Top Hunter. His groom? A teenager from Maryland called David

O'Connor. We were soon to hear a lot more from both of them in international eventing.

In more ways than one, the reverberations from Kentucky 1978 would continue for some time to come.

13

Badminton and Burghley and the Olympic Games— Oh My!

In 1979, the Pan Am Games were held in Puerto Rico, and there was no three-day event scheduled. Believing as I do that there is no substitute for experience in international competition, and with the Moscow Olympics only a year away, I asked the USET to allocate grants to each rider selected to assist with the trip to Badminton instead. This was a new move for the USET, and incidentally, this formula has been used extensively since then as it is much less expensive than sending a full team on a European tour. Five riders were able to make the trip. Four were sponsored by the team: Jim Wofford and Carawich, Derek di Grazia and Thriller II, Karen Lende and March Brown, and Karen Reuter Sachey with High Kite. Jim was by now a veteran USET rider, but the other three were exciting young prospects who had started to make a name for themselves in national competition. The fifth, a young rider named Wash Bishop with his horse Jones, traveled as an individual and was billed separately. Even though Wash was not sponsored by the USET, I included him as a full member and treated him just like the team-sponsored riders throughout the competition. Thriller II was injured before the start of the competition, and Karen Sachey was eliminated in the show jumping. Karen Lende and March Brown finished in 10th, and it was left to Jim Wofford to secure a fourth place on Carawich. The competition was won for the fourth time by Lucinda Prior-Palmer riding Killaire. Lucinda was to go on to six Badminton titles on six different horses, a record that has not only stood for many years but will surely stand for many to come.

THE FIRST AND ONLY PROTEST

Wash Bishop had a very controversial elimination after the dressage. Jones was questionably sound on the turns during his dressage test, but the jury did not ring the bell as was required by the rules at the time and his score was posted on the scoreboard. According to the rules at the time, the horse could not be examined nor eliminated by the Ground Jury until he was back in competition during the endurance test. Instead of following this rule, the Ground Jury asked one of the stable vets to examine the horse and then report to the Ground Jury. The vet examined the horse in the stable, reported to the Ground Jury and they eliminated the horse.

This was the first and only time in my long career as a chef d'equipe that I lodged a protest as there were several elements of the procedure that violated the rules. I also had to lodge a protest because of the unwillingness of the Ground Jury to accept my suggestion to jog the horse in front of the Ground Jury with the Ground Jury veterinarian. That was turned down, which led me to file a written protest.

In my written protest, I again offered to accept their decision if the horse was examined in front of the Ground Jury by the Ground Jury veterinarian. The Ground Jury turned down my offer and confirmed their decision to eliminate Jones. My only option was to appeal. In those days, the Jury of Appeal had the power and duty to receive appeals and act on them. I was then contacted by the Technical Delegate who asked me to withdraw my appeal since the President of the Appeal Committee was the Duke of Beaufort, and he had to prepare to receive the Queen and didn't have time to hear my appeal. I could not see myself accepting that excuse and not defend the interest of my rider, and immediately refused. Finally, the Jury of Appeal found the time to meet and consider the appeal, but in my presence, it was quite quickly denied so everyone could go back to their more important social activities.

That was it. Jones was eliminated. After Badminton, Mr. Pip Graham, Jones' owner, and I, wrote a letter to the FEI stating the numerous articles under which the rules were violated. The FEI wrote back to Mr. Graham, Wash, and me as chef d'equipe to say they were sorry because the Badminton organization made a mistake, and that a letter would be sent to Badminton reprimanding them. At the same time, the FEI asked us to be satisfied with the apology and not to exploit the incident in the media.

Probably as a consequence of this incident, the rule was changed. As it stands today, if a horse's soundness is questionable in the dressage test then the Ground Jury has the option to ask the Ground Jury vet to examine the horse and report to the President of the Ground Jury. If the vet considers the horse lame, the whole Ground Jury and the vet must examine the horse together before making a decision.

We were back in England again that fall for Burghley, Britain's other major three-day event. Torrance Watkins had Red's Door and Poltroon entered. Red's Door had an uphill battle making the time on the course, which looked deceptively soft but was not, and finished in 21st. The unbelievable little pinto mare Poltroon wowed the crowds and with Torrance blazed home into second place. Andrew Hoy's Davey was in the lead after cross-country by a whisker and it came down to a hair-raising finish when, with Poltroon clear in the show jumping, Davey, having just 1.6 penalties in hand, rattled a good many of the rails. However, he got away without actually dropping a pole to win, leaving the 15.1 hand mare in second place. We were all ecstatic at this performance and knew we had a new team horse for Moscow.

1980 FONTAINEBLEAU – ALTERNATIVE OLYMPICS

In 1980, world politics once again impacted the scheduled Olympic Games in Moscow when the Russians invaded Afghanistan. In protest, many countries boycotted the Moscow Games, which made that competition less of an Olympic Games and more of a competition between Eastern Block countries. In the 1970s and 1980s, world politics had an immense and often devastating and tragic effect on the Olympic Games which, given the whole philosophy of the Olympic movement, is a sad indictment of human nature.

The FEI decided that all those nations who boycotted the Olympic Three-Day Event could compete in an international CCIO (Concours Complet International Officiel) at Fontainebleau in France.

The major eventing nations all went to Fontainebleau including Argentina, Australia, Belgium, Britain, Canada, France, Germany, Holland, Ireland, and Italy. The home team of Joel Pons (Ensorceleuse), Jean-Yves Touzaint (Flipper), Thierry Touzaint (Gribouille), and Armand Bigot (Gamin du Bois) won the team gold medal with Denmark's Nils Haagensen taking the individual gold medal on the Thoroughbred-Hanoverian cross, Monaco.

French organizers rose to the occasion and in just three months put on a superb event at Fontainebleau, a beautiful chateau that had been the residence of several kings and the Emperor Napoleon. This competition came to be called eventing's "Alternative Olympics."

The US sent a team of four and two individuals. The team was made up of Jim Wofford on Carawich, Torrance Watkins and Poltroon, Mike Plumb and Laurenson, and Mike Huber and Gold Chip. The two individuals were Karen Stives and The Saint, and Wash Bishop and Taxi.

The team was lying in second place after dressage, and I knew we had a chance of improving on that after walking the cross-country. The course was very demanding being very winding with lots of turns. Every fence required a big, bold effort or technical accuracy.

The severity of the cross-country was evidenced by the number of falls; in fact, there were falls at 30 of the 34 fences on the course with the water responsible for six of that number.

The first US rider out was Wash Bishop on Taxi. Competing as an individual, Wash had to report back on how the course was riding. Unfortunately, Taxi had two falls that resulted in his elimination. The next day we found that Taxi had developed a fever and a virus which accounted for him being unable to perform to his usual standard. Ill fortune was to befall the team also.

As the cross-country progressed, we moved up with every horse until we were in the lead by 90 points! An unassailable lead I hear you say. After our third horse, Gold Chip, came home I was worried. Gold Chip's knee looked bad as she had sustained a deep cut. I asked Marty Simensen to go back to the stable and check her out and give me his opinion as to what her chances were of show jumping the next day. Marty came back with the news that although Gold Chip would be fine in a few days, there was no chance of her being fit to show jump. So, it was down to Mike Plumb and Laurenson to secure the team gold medal for the US.

Mike's instructions were to go for a safe clear round and do everything he could to ensure that we had a team to show jump the next day. That is a lot of pressure! Now Mike is one of the greatest riders of all time, a superb team member, and I think of him as a dear friend, but on this occasion, he had what I would call today a "brain fart." All riders in this position clearly understand that in the event of a refusal at a fence with an alternative route they are to immediately take the longer and easier option to minimize the risk of any further penalties.

At this point in the competition, with the US in such a dominant position, Mike could have taken every long route on the course, had he wanted to. He had a fantastic round and was foot perfect coming into the second to last fence, a significant water complex. If Laurenson had a weakness, it was water jumps and his successful competition record was due to the rider on his back. I was standing near the water jump feeling quite confident that we would finish the day well in the lead when Laurenson came into the first element and refused. Oh well, we had the 20 penalties well in hand, Mike would take the option, and we would be okay, thought I. But no, Mike approached the fence again at the same place, and again Laurenson refused. Now he would take the option; our lead was greatly diminished but we could still do it. In utter amazement and disbelief, I watched Mike turn again, approach the fence in exactly the same spot as the previous two times, and get eliminated for a third refusal. The team's chances of a medal were gone, and it was left to Jim Wofford and Torrance Watkins to win the silver and bronze medals for the US as individuals.

For two days I couldn't even look at Mike, let alone speak to him.

On the third day, he came to me and asked, "When are you going to let me have it, Coach?" To ask what he had been thinking would have been stupid and futile. It was apparent that his thinking capacity had eluded him that day, and no thought process had occurred whatsoever. There was also a factor of a romance going on that could explain this complete brain fart on Mike's part. (As an example, Mike Huber had taken an option with the injured Gold Chip on cross-country and managed to complete the course!)

But I was wrong. "I'm sorry Jack, I honestly thought I could get him over it," was Mike's reply. Perhaps he could have done so if the rules allowed for that many attempts!

The annual Luhmuhlen CCI in Germany was the weekend after Fontainebleau and some of the US alternative horses were to compete there. Mike had Better and Better entered but after the fiasco at Fontainebleau, he felt so bad about himself that he just wanted to go home to the States. Better and Better was ready to run, and I was not going to let Mike back out. I finally was able to convince him to compete and hoped things were going to go well. I do not know what was going on in Mike's head at this particular time, but he made another big mistake by violating one of the rules on saddlery in the warm-up area before the competition. Fortunately, one of our riders saw him and tried to convince him that was not allowed. When Mike refused to change, the rider ran to tell me and I ran to the warm-up area. I was terribly, terribly mad at him, as mad as I have ever been. I told him, "When stupidity fell upon the earth, you certainly did not have an umbrella!" His explanation to me was that he could not find the rule change in the rule book. This was because the rule had just recently been changed and why we had talked about it the night before!

Still, life goes on, and guess what? Mike and Better and Better won the Luhmuhlen CCI. Oh my!

14

LUHMUHLEN AND LOS ANGELES

Kim Walnes and The Gray Goose began to hit the top of the score-boards in 1980. In 1981, an International Invitational was run at Kentucky as well as an Advanced level three-day event. Kim and "Gray" placed second in the Advanced division and put themselves on the list for a trip to Germany later in the year. She proved her worth there by finishing a very respectable 10th so by the time I was looking for riders for the World Championships in Luhmuhlen in 1982, Kim and The Gray Goose were solid prospects for a medal. We were scheduled to ship out to Compiegne, France to complete our training, and three days before we left Kim had a fall in the show-jumping arena and broke two of the transverse processes (part of the vertebrae) in her back. One doctor told her she was not allowed to ride for six weeks, and when I looked at the calendar, I saw that put us three weeks out from the Worlds. That was cutting it very close. She and the horse had been very successful, and she knew him inside and out, and he did her, so against all logical thinking, I kept the pair on the list to go to Germany even though people said I was nuts to do this. I rode the horse on the flat every day and did some show jumping on him, but I got Mike Plumb to gallop him and take him out schooling cross-country jumps to keep him in top condition. One day we were schooling jumps, and I asked Mike to take the horse through the bounce. The Gray Goose came up to the bounce and promptly put in a stride. I told Mike to jump another fence and come around again and make him bounce it this time. Round he came and the horse insisted on putting in a stride again. No matter what Mike did the horse always put in a stride. After three attempts I said let's stop there. Kim was by my side while the horse was jumping and said, "Mike doesn't talk to him. He has to tell him it's a bounce. If he doesn't tell him, he won't know!" Kim talked to the horse all the time she was riding him and truly believed he understood her. I went over to Mike and told him that he had to talk to the horse! Mike was not convinced that a lack of verbal communication was the problem. And neither was I!

Kim was on the mend, and she was riding on the flat a little bit and wanted to try jumping. So when we were training in the arena one afternoon, I set up show jumps in an replica of the cross-country bounce as far as height and distances were concerned. She came up to the fence, ba da boom, ba da boom, ba da boom, all the while talking to the horse. "Now this is a bounce that you are going to jump okay? This is a bounce." The Gray Goose went right through the combination perfectly, jump, land, jump! Kim turned to Mike and me and said, "You see it's easy when you tell him what to expect." I thought Mike was going to eat his whip.

The Gray Goose went to the World Championships in Luhmuhlen and jumped Kim around clean and fast to win the individual bronze medal for herself and in doing so helped the United States win the team bronze.

RETIREMENT LOOMS

In 1982, I told Bill Steinkraus that I was going to retire after the 1984 Los Angeles Olympic Games. Bill, an Olympic gold medalist in show jumping, was then president of the US Equestrian Team. He asked me if it was a matter of more money and whether a higher salary would change my mind, but it wasn't and it wouldn't. I was tired. I had been coaching since 1965, almost 20 years and although I had great support for what I was doing from my wife Madeleine, I had not had any real family life. My daughter Corinne had once said to Madeleine, "Let's have a party, Father's home." My being home was a very special occasion in her mind and that hurt. Most fathers come home to their children nearly every night. I was there so rarely they wanted to have a party to celebrate. It made me think long and hard. I was not just gone for one or two weeks; sometimes I was gone three, four, six months at a time. Madeleine did an excellent job of raising Florence and Corinne on her own. She had created a life for herself and the girls without me, and when I came home, I had the feeling that I disrupted that life and that was very hard for me to accept.

At home, I was the Director of the Training Center with all that entailed, and when we traveled I was coach, chef d'equipe, trainer, travel agent, accountant, and I got tired of doing it alone. Oh yes, at home I had a stable manager and Patrick, who now had oversight of all the maintenance and upkeep of the training center at Gladstone. Thankfully he also helped me with organizing transportation, setting up jumps and so on, but he no longer traveled with me. I was also lucky to have two secretaries in the office, but on the road it was all down to me. The riders, who all had grooms, simply had to check the roster to see what time they were scheduled for lessons, then turn up and get on their horses. Everything was done for them.

Today, there are a number of people doing the job I did. Captain Mark Phillips became chef d'equipe of the US Team in 1993. The position no longer included all the logistical and housekeeping jobs expected of a full-time coach in the seventies and eighties. I had all of the horses full time once the team was picked and made sure that veterinary instructions were carried out to the letter. On the road I ordered the hay and grain, hired the farrier, and arranged stabling. I had a letter of credit for $50,000, and I had to account for every penny.

I had to make sure that the riders attended all the social functions to promote the sport and fulfill sponsor/owner requirements. I had five riders, five grooms, a stable manager, and the vet to oversee and make all travel arrangements for and this wasn't for just a week or two; it was often many months. On the long trips I would send the riders home, and while they were away, I would keep their horses in training myself. While I liked them all, I was still the coach, and that can be a very lonely job. I never had a day off, and I just got downright tired. I taught lessons all day, group lessons for jumping and individual lessons in dressage and I had no time for any kind of life other than being the coach. One rider every day was assigned the responsibility for posting the schedule and communicating with all the other riders and grooms. At night, I prepared the schedule for each day after I had performed my clerical duties. I think the system worked well but eventually the pace started to take its toll, and I realized that I could not keep this up forever.

When I broached the matter with Bill, it was with the intention of helping the team prepare for my departure. I planned to give them sufficient time to find a replacement coach who would then work with me and ease into the position ready to take over after Los Angeles. It came as something of a surprise then when Bill told me not to say a word about this to anyone. He told me that I did not understand the American mentality and that once I announced that I was leaving, I would in effect lose all my influence and authority. More than that, it appeared that the riders did not believe they needed a coach and that they could manage by themselves. I didn't believe him and said that there was no way they could manage without a coach, no team could, but he simply said, "Trust me, Jack, these guys think they are good enough and can do it by themselves." I decided to make no mystery of the fact that I would be leaving after the Games and the last weeks leading to Los Angeles were the toughest times of my career. In retrospect, Bill was right, and I should have followed his advice.

SILENT PARTNER

One high spot during this time was a bet I had with Karen Stives. She had a lovely horse called Silent Partner with whom she had had some success, but neither she nor I felt he would be a consistent team horse. He had a very good base of dressage, as Karen had begun her riding career in that discipline, and would have been successful in that sport if she had not lost her heart to eventing. At home in Hamilton, I was riding Silent Partner for her on the flat and happened to mention that it wouldn't take long to turn him into a dressage horse and teach him piaffe and passage. She didn't believe me, and so I asked her if she wanted to bet on it. She did. I asked how much time she would give me, and she said three months. I said, "What about three weeks?" She was doubtful it could be done and especially so when I told her that under the terms of the bet I would not use spurs, nor a double bridle and I would do it all from the saddle, no ground work. If I did it, I wanted a case of top-class champagne delivered to my house; if I didn't, then she would get the champagne. Well, Karen could almost taste that champagne.

I rode the horse twice a day, and I worked him everywhere and any-where, on the grass behind the mansion, on the front lawn of the mansion out on the racetrack and by two and a half weeks I felt I was almost there. One day I caught Karen peeping round the corner of the mansion watching me. She thought I might be using some tricks and was following me hiding from tree to tree because she did not believe I could get that horse into passage without some trick training. Three weeks later I asked her to go with me onto the front lawn and told her I was going to passage Silent Partner one time around the ring. Karen had the champagne delivered to my door that night! Shortly afterward, a young equitation rider came to try him, and she showed him in passage and also demonstrated his flying changes. He was bought that day and went to Madison Square Garden not long afterward.

GAMES OF CONTENTION

There were five riders in training for Los Angeles, and only four would be named to the team with one being named the reserve. The pressure and tension were almost unbearable. This was not just the Olympic Games; it was the Olympic Games on US soil. The riders now had owners and sponsors and were desperate to justify all the money that had been invested in them and the horses. Not only that, they knew their future security rested on a successful performance on an Olympic Team. It would have a great impact on their future professional businesses. I could understand it, but living with it was extremely hard.

One evening, I noticed two unknown gentlemen in the stables and enquired what they were doing there at this late hour. One replied that he had been hired to protect one of the rider's horses. Of course, only Team members could have benefited from that particular horse being unable to compete in Los Angeles, but it demonstrated the level of stress that the riders were under. There is no doubt that the atmosphere was more tense than I had ever experienced before and with my pending retirement, I felt that it did not bode well for the future. Of course, Madeleine was standing beside me 100 percent and all that support allowed me to stand fast during that very challenging and stressful period of my professional life.

Riders got very edgy with each other, and I felt that the team spirit was just not there. Jeanne Kane was the stable manager then, and she was a good friend to me as was Patrick. Their loyal support was precious to me during these difficult times, and I will never forget them.

Overall, from eventing's perspective, Los Angeles was a contentious Olympic Games from the start. Neil Ayer was named as the organizer for equestrian sports and was also the course designer at Fairbanks. While the dressage and show jumping took place at the Santa Anita Racetrack, the speed and endurance phases were a two-hour drive south to the Fairbanks Golf Course. Differences of opinion arose within the organizing body, and when it became apparent that Neil could not work in that environment, he stepped down from his organizing duties and concentrated on designing the course. The public never knew of all the high drama taking place in the background.

As the history books tell, the event was a huge success for the United States who took the team gold. Karen Stives was standing in the gold medal slot going into show jumping and would drop to second with one rail down. Two would have relegated the team to silver. Twenty-seven-year-old Mark Todd and the little Charisma put on all the pressure with a clear round even if he did touch every single one of the rails with his toes. Mark later described Charisma's show-jumping round as "jumping by Braille." Karen and Ben Arthur dropped the middle part of the combination for five penalties, which dropped them into the silver-medal position and moved Mark up to gold. Karen's performance, though, kept the team in the lead and once again I was lucky enough to have coached an Olympic gold medal team. It was the perfect time for me to move on.

28. Walking the course with the 1976 Olympic Team. L–R: Mary Anne Tauskey; Bruce Davidson; Mike Plumb (always thinking); and Tad striding the distance.
Photo by Barry Kaplan/TFI Photo.

29. I believe this is the only photograph in existence of the three Olympic coaches in Montreal. All three disciplines brought home medals. L–R: Bert de Némethy, Bengt Ljungquist, and Jack Le Goff.
Photo courtesy of US Equestrian Archives.

30. I love this picture of Tad and Bally Cor. The mare is thinking and going forward and Tad is right where he belongs in the saddle.

Photo by Barry Kaplan/TFI Photo.

31. The 1980 Alternative Olympic Teams meet the President. Jimmy and Rosalind Carter and their daughter Amy welcomed all the Olympic equestrian teams to the White House. Front row: President Jimmy Carter; First Lady Rosalind Carter; Amy Carter. Second row L–R: Terri Rudd; Linda Zang; Jack Burton; Melle Von Bruggen; Third row L–R: Jim Wofford; Melanie Smith; Karen Stives; Gwen Stockebrand; Torrance Watkins; JLG. Back row L–R: Wash Bishop; Norman Dello Joio; Lendon Gray; Katie Monahan (now Prudent), Mike Plumb; John Winnett (hiding behind me).

*With best wishes
to Jack Le Goff*

Jimmy Carter

32. Shaking hands with the President and Mrs. Carter.

33. I was honored with the prestigious Horseman of the Year Award in 1983, which I received from Mr. McDevitt the president of the AHSA. *Photo Courtesy of US Equestrian Archives.*

34. Working on the flat with a true professional—Karen Stives and The Saint. Karen's face exhibits the dedication and concentration that was her hallmark.

35. At Ledyard with my great friend Neil Ayer who designed both the 1984 Los Angeles Olympic course and the 1986 Gawler World Championship course. *Photo by Fifi Coles.*

36. At an instructor's seminar with some very famous riders. L–R: JLG, Anne Kursinski, Michael Page, and George Morris.

37. This photo went on the front cover of the *USCTA News*. *Photo by Fifi Coles.*

38. It was a joy to ride this horse. I am perfecting the shoulder-in on Rob Stevenson's Risky Business during the weeks leading up to the Barcelona Olympics. This horse was the best of the Canadians in Spain. *Photo by SLMS.*

39. One of my other loves: Fishing for blue fish off the coast of Massachusetts with show jumper Julie Ulrich and fellow Frenchman Christian Meunier. Christian was the head of the import and export agency for top sport horses in France. Julie now also lives in France where she buys and sells international jumpers and event horses. *Photo by Florence Le Goff.*

40. And my other love hunting: Here I am on my only attempt at elk hunting in Colorado with my friend Hans Henzi. People dined well that week. We had to use a "come along" to load this big elk. *Photo by SLMS.*

41. I was asked to conduct a series of clinics in Australia in 1991. I'm with Kevin Bacon the famous show jumper and my good friend. *Photo by SLMS.*

42. It wasn't all work when I went to New Zealand to teach a series of clinics. I spent a good day with my dear Susan fishing for (and as you can see we caught) wild trout. *Photo by SLMS.*

43. I was the guest of honor on a wild boar shoot held by the King of Morocco. Here I am with a member of the French Olympic team in Mexico, Jean-Louis Martin. He has been responsible for breeding horses for the Moroccan royal family for 35 years.

44. At my happiest in my preferred outfit—a 6-pound bass. *Photo by SLMS.*

45. In Aachen, 2006 with my former student, dear friend and 2000 Olympic gold medalist David O'Connor. I had just spent nine days in a German hospital suffering from a serious infection. *Photo copyright © 2006 Nancy Jaffer.*

46. The winner of the dressage at Rolex Kentucky, the final selection trial for the 1980 Games in Fontainebleau. Torrance Watkins executes an exceptional extended trot on the brilliant little Poltroon. *Photo by Findlay Davidson.*

47. With one of my favorite people, Jim Wofford at Badminton in 1979.
Photo by Sue Maynard.

48. A treasured photograph. With my dearest friend and brother Pierre in front of the Hare and Hounds at Badminton in 1965. This photo was the last one taken of us together. He died in a car accident just a few weeks later.
Photo by Jean Bridel.

49. Colonel Margot did this painting of me racing. He was a phenomenal horseman and the chief écuyer at the Cadre Noir and a wonderful artist.

Le capitaine Rémiat
montant Coup droit (P.S.A.).
Technique mixte.
31 x 22,5 cm.

50. My dear friend Jacques Remiat riding Coup droit. On this horse Jacques competed in grand prix dressage, advanced eventing, and show jumping and was part of the dressage quadrille—all at the same time!

51. H.R.H. The Infanta Doña Pilar De Borbón—President of the FEI from 1994 to 2006.

52. Mike Plumb and Better and Better at Blue Ridge Horse Trials.

With the greatest admiration, respect and thanks of Bruce & "Irish Cap"

53. Bruce Davidson and Irish Cap.

54. I'm riding the Arizona range with Susan and two of my closest friends from France, Professor Dominique Roualec and Jacques Remiat.
Photo by Patricia Motley.

15

A NEW AND DIFFERENT ROLE

Ah, retirement! Long lazy days of meditation by the lake with a fishing rod in my hand. A day's hunting with my gun, my friends and my faithful Labrador at my side. Maybe one day but not yet. Though I did not want to coach the US Team any longer, there was no doubt that I was going to stay in the equestrian profession, and likely in eventing, but it would be on a private basis. In other words, doing what I had been doing all along, but with less stress and more time at home.

I may have retired as team coach in 1984, but I was not ready to spend the rest of my life in gentle contemplation. With my work for the USET Olympic Three-Day Team at its end, my professional life took a turn toward private teaching. I conducted many clinics in the US and abroad including France, Germany, Australia, New Zealand, and Mexico. I was doing a fair amount of FEI judging in different parts of the world and also took on the technical director job of the FEI competition in Chantilly, France. It was a very busy life, but I enjoyed it.

I also continued to conduct clinics in all parts of the United States. I wanted to concentrate on the Western states where training sessions took place regularly at Wild Horse Valley Ranch in the Napa Valley. The idea was to help the West Coast riders to have their own programs without necessarily having to go to the East Coast to train and compete.

My good friend Andrew Popiel ran the ill-fated Trojan Horse Trials in Cave Creek, Arizona. I say ill-fated because it was one of the most valuable horse trials in the country, and one fundamental to the growth of the sport in the West, yet it was threatened annually by rampant development (a threat to which it finally succumbed in April 2002). Beginning in the 1970s, I used to give clinics at Andrew's ranch. He had built a lot of cross-country jumps and one day he and I picked an area where one could see a lot of obstacles from one vantage spot, and I made some suggestions for complexes that he could use for clinics as well as competitions. On my next trip to Trojan, Andrew took me out on his golf cart and showed me a big red and yellow sign. It said, "Le Goff's Amusement Park"!

Even though I had retired, Bill Steinkraus and I were in discussions about the future of the US Team and what would constitute success in the years to come. We decided that I should also stay on as Director of the USET Training Center in Hamilton, Massachusetts. There I would be responsible for the Young Rider Development Program which, in essence, meant I would continue to search for and develop new young riders. We found an acceptable arrangement satisfying both parties, and life went on.

I shall say, though, that while the Team and I were satisfied with our new situation, some senior riders were not. They wanted the money marked for the development program spent exclusively on themselves. Most of those riders had benefited themselves from that very program. Did they not want the younger generation to have the same privilege? Well, I guess it is human nature.

I proceeded to look out for up-and-coming riders through some of the talent-spotting clinics I conducted. Just as I had done when I was the coach, I invited a few of the ones that caught my eye to come to Hamilton as resident riders. One of those was my last resident rider, David O'Connor. Finding riders such as David justified the program I had developed as well as all of the effort and financial support from the USET.

THE SHOW JUMPING TALENT DERBY

The center had a lovely big indoor arena and a beautiful expanse of lawn in front of the Clark mansion. There were some very interesting features on that lawn, including a multi-faceted bank, ditches, and a water jump. I thought we could make some good use of these and so in 1985 or so I started a Show Jumping Talent Derby. It was designed to showcase the jumping skills of young riders under the age of 25. To compete, they must never have ridden in the Olympics or World Championships or more than three times on a Nations Cup team.

The competition attracted a large number of spectators year after year. They came to watch these talented young riders jump a Derby course and to support the USET. The Derby consisted of three classes: a qualifying class Saturday; the Derby itself where the 25 top riders would compete on Sunday afternoon; and the consolation class where the remaining riders would compete on Sunday morning. The winners, most of whom would go on to represent the United States on Olympic and World Championships teams, took home $50,000 in prize money, which in those days was an attractive sum of money. The showground and course were beautifully decorated with a tremendous amount of flowers thanks to the ladies of the local community. We were also able to turn in quite a handsome check to the USET every year to help fund international competition.

I liked the idea of a Derby course that is so common in Europe versus the show jumping held in a stadium because there are natural fences, for example, ditches, banks, drops, and water jumps and it is not always held on flat ground. In fact, in the US show jumping is often referred to as stadium jumping.

I have strong recollections of Bert de Némethy trying to compensate for the lack of experience of horses and riders over natural fences by having special schooling in the upper field at Gladstone over water jumps. Our riders turned in clear rounds over the rails but often had four faults in the *rivière* when going to Europe.

COACHING CANADA

The USET and I had an agreement that I would devote two-thirds of my time to the team development program and one-third of my time to the development of my own professional business. In 1990, the Canadians approached me to help train their team. I had helped them part time for the World Equestrian Games in Stockholm in 1990, and they now asked me to coach the team for the 1991 Pan Am Games and the 1992 Barcelona Olympics.

The Pan American Games were to be held in Cuba, not terribly famous for its three-day eventing facilities which, to put it bluntly, are non-existent. So, Belgian rider and businessman Carl Bouckaert, one of the most stalwart supporters of eventing in the United States offered his Georgia farm for the three-day event championships. At that time the Pan Am Games were held at the equivalent of a CCI** today. The Games upgraded to a CCIO*** a little later following the reorganization of the star system by the FEI. Up until that time all Advanced three-day events were categorized as three-stars including Badminton, Burghley, and the Olympic and World Games. The sheer difficulty of these competitions set them apart from all others, and the general thinking internationally was that a four-star level would both recognize the high standard and complexity of the events and reward the riders and horses who completed them successfully by offering a higher level of points and thus acknowledging their achievements.

Nick Holmes-Smith was then 34. He had represented Canada in two Olympics, Fontainebleau (1980) and Seoul (1988) and two World

Equestrian Games, Luhmuhlen (1982), and Stockholm (1990). He was riding the gray Canadian-bred Thoroughbred/Quarter Horse Ruderpest, owned by Paul Popiel, brother of Andrew. Ruderpest got his name from a song from My Fair Lady when the character sings, "Every time we turned around, there he was, that hairy hound from Budapest. Never have I known a ruder pest."

Stuart Black and Von Perrier, Edie Tarves-Gourlay with Socrates, and Jamie Smart and Glendevlin made up the rest of the team, which was to give me one of the great thrills of my "retirement" by winning the team gold medal. Nick and Ruderpest won the individual gold after leading from the dressage.

Those Pan Am Games will linger in my memory for a long time if only for the weather. It was freezing, with temperatures hovering between 20 and 30 degrees and the wind blowing violently. The tack shops sold out because people had not brought enough warm clothes and more importantly did not have enough blankets for their horses. Such are the vagaries of the Georgia climate.

One of the young Canadians that I had the pleasure to work with during that period was Rob Stevenson and his horse Risky Business. Rob missed the Pan Am selection and had begun to train for the Barcelona Olympics. The horse needed careful preparation, and if not handled right, he would be unsound. He was a superb horse cross-country and his show jumping was good, so we kept that part of the preparation to a minimum. In fact, as I recall we only jumped him twice in the lead-up to Barcelona and the majority of the conditioning was done through a mix of dressage work and swimming. I had come to appreciate the benefits of swimming horses when we were trying to minimize the impact of the fast work on Bally Cor back in the seventies, and now Risky Business reinforced its value as he began to get fitter and fitter without the pounding on those legs and feet. I even began to think that eventing could be a real triathlon of the horse if we added a swimming phase!

Barcelona '92

And so, in 1992 I was back in the routine of selection trials and training sessions. The Barcelona Olympics were significant for a number of reasons. The cross-country course was elevated to new heights both in terms of design and expense, and it was the last Olympics to give two medals for one performance. The high temperatures of a Spanish summer combined with the complexity of the course created an almost impossible challenge for many of the horses and the resulting falls provided the media, and in particular television, with sufficient material to almost get the sport shut down.

There was an enormous public outcry about the perceived inhumane treatment of event horses to the extent that the Humane Society of the United States turned its attention to the sport and called for changes to be made. It was made very clear that eventing would now take center stage but not for the reasons we had all wished.

The Australians and the New Zealanders, thanks to the superb preparation of their horses and the experience of their riders, came out of it all with the gold and the silver medals and Matt Ryan and Kibah Tic Toc won the individual gold. Herbert Blocker and that great mare, Feine Dame, took the silver, and Blyth Tait and Messiah took the bronze. Blyth and Messiah had suffered through a disastrous dressage test that left them in 69th place, but their incredible ability in both of the jumping phases saw them soar up the standings and take the bronze medal. Thinking back on Messiah's performance, I have to ask myself if our sport in the 21st century will allow us to see a feat like that repeated.

As it turned out, Rob Stevenson and Risky Business were able to pace themselves nicely throughout that long, hot cross-country course and finished the day with 0.8 time penalties on the steeplechase and 47.6 time penalties on the course. The other team members for Canada were King Plantagenet and Rachel Hunter, Sir

Lancelot and Nick Holmes-Smith, and Von Perrier ridden by Stuart Black. Rachel and Nick placed forty-ninth and fifty-third respectively, and Von Perrier gave me another "first", but this one I didn't want. In all of my years of coaching teams, I have never, ever had a horse excluded at the final inspection. At Barcelona, Von Perrier, after being jogged about eight times for the Ground Jury, was spun, which caused great disappointment to Stuart and me.

There was no doubt about it, though: the FEI and the entire international eventing community were on alert. Atlanta, just four years away, was going to be just as hot, and a lot more humid than Barcelona. The sport was undergoing changes and in Atlanta, we would see for the first time both team and individual competitions. While this answered those critics who were complaining that eventing was being given two medals for one performance, it did nothing to answer those who said that the Olympic three-day event was far too expensive and required too much land and too many volunteers.

MOVING ON

For me, though, the coaching days were done forever. I would continue to fulfill my obligations as an international judge and would work on any committees the FEI appointed me to, but no more would I be persuaded to coach. I believe I was the longest lasting chef d'equipe and coach in eventing, having served in that role from 1965 to 1992.

At this juncture, the USET changed their policy and elected not to have a full-time coach anymore. They further decided that the Gladstone, New Jersey, facility would be sufficient to gather and train the teams before going abroad as well as host training sessions and clinics for all the various disciplines. Consequently, they decided to close down the Hamilton training center at the end of 1992. They offered to bring me to Gladstone, but I did not wish to return. I had a home in Hamilton, but I no longer had a job with the USET. Simultaneously, Madeleine and I, as great friends and with immense respect for one another, decided to go our separate ways. We sold the house and Madeleine went back to France with my two daughters, and I moved down to Virginia.

In 1993, I bought a condominium in Carefree, Arizona, where I was spending so much time conducting clinics. I also purchased a town-house in Saumur, France. The Saumur house was a place to hang my hat when visiting Europe for all types of horse activities, as well as being close to my French family. It was a move that took me back to my roots and gave me an opportunity to see all my old friends from the Cadre Noir. My mother was in her mid-nineties and, being the only child left it was important that I spend as much time as possible with her.

Having the house in Arizona made it very easy to spend time there in the winter months teaching and giving clinics at Andrew's ranch. It was a pleasure working at Andrew's and the large variety of banks, ditches and water jumps that he had built made it ideal for training both horses and riders. We set up annual training sessions during the weeks leading up to the two early spring Trojan Horse Ranch Horse Trials. Riders came from all over the western United States and from Canada and stayed for two weeks of clinics, which culmi-nated in the horse trials. The schedule worked out very well, and I would only take eight riders in the whole two-week clinic, which allowed for some serious work to be done. It was there that I first set eyes on a young girl whom I thought would be one of the future superstars of eventing. Her name was Kimberly Severson. I remem-ber during one lecture I asked the riders individually what they wanted to do in the horse business in the future. When it came to Kim's turn, she looked me straight in the eyes and said, "I am going to ride in the Olympics!" I looked back at her and thought, "Sure young lady, you and 250 others."

But as the clinic went on I realized that this young woman not only had talent but she had tremendous determination and a quality rare to find in young riders—she had the power of concentration.

During 1992-93 I gave her a horse of mine to ride and suggested she move east to work out of Morven Park where I was based at the time. I would teach her, and she would ride my mare. This worked out well until a stable management mistake led me to end our arrangement. I knew that she had the ability to go all the way and achieve her goal, and she sure did. She is one of the most talented natural riders that I have seen in my long career, and I enjoyed watching her ride. I am proud to say I am a charter member of her "fan club."

It was about this time that a very special person came into my life. A few years before, a young lady by the name of Crys Withington, who worked with me in Hamilton as stable manager, introduced me to a very attractive and charming woman by the name of Susan Miller-Smith. When I first met Susan, Crys and I were at the Radnor Three-Day Event, and Susan had a tack shop in the trade fair. I was very attracted to her, but it went no further at the time. The years passed and one day my friend Crys, being a neighbor of Susan's, encouraged her to invite me to a shooting party at her farm. The evening spent at Susan's was memorable thanks to the great food, good wine, and the excellent company.

Another of my special friends and a pupil, Courtney Ramsay, was with me at the time, and after we left, I could not get this beautiful, intelligent, and charming lady out of my mind. Courtney and I were on a tour of the United States in an RV, trying to get in as much fishing, shooting, and beautiful scenery as we could in the southern part of the country. I am sure Courtney quickly had enough of hearing about this lady with whom I was falling in love.

I sent Susan a thank you note for her hospitality, saying that it was probably poor form to fall in love with the hostess of the party, but that was what had happened. More years went by and the next time we met was at Dressage at Devon, and that was IT! This time, I can use the word instant. It was instant love, just like instant coffee and fortunately for me the same thing happened to Susan. For 15 years, she has been the center of my life; she captured my heart, my soul, and my body. Susan traveled the world with me and became my constant companion. She never tired of the judging trips or the clinics and instead threw herself into my work, helping me schedule my commitments and organize my clinics among so many other things.

PART III

THE FEI YEARS

"I believe that you have to be very serious when you officiate, as long as you don't take yourself too seriously when you're not officiating!"

16

JUDGING

I was already judging some events before I came to the United States. My first international judging job was at Wylie in 1974 for Lord and Lady Russell. I became an FEI judge in 1975 and gradually worked my way to the "O" status. In the early 1970s I held US judging licenses in dressage, eventing, and jumping. I dropped the jumping license because you have to judge hunters and equitation, and I knew nothing about those disciplines. I was kept pretty busy with those sports I knew about. It would have been a waste for me to take up a seat that was much better filled by an expert in that discipline.

Around 1971, I was appointed to the American Horse Shows Association (AHSA) (now the US Equestrian Federation) Dressage and Eventing committees. I soon dropped the Dressage Committee because there is only so much one can do, but I kept my US dressage license along with my FEI dressage license.

Today at the FEI level there is something in the order of 200 events a year, which require an enormous amount of officials. Not so back when I started! At that time, the FEI amounted to a few Army colonels and generals who were retired, could afford to go to a couple of events a year, and were honored to judge without compensation. There were no lists of course designers and technical delegates so when it came to organizing events you had to be very creative and pretty much the axiom was: if you want something done then do it yourself. Today there is a book of almost 200 pages listing all of the FEI officials in the various disciplines from all over the world. This accomplishment is something of which the FEI can be proud.

A judge should keep his sense of humor. Mine was challenged twice. On the first occasion at the end of the competition, the rider came down the centerline of the dressage ring with a wheelbarrow and a bag of dog food in it. He halted at "G" in front of the President Judge's booth, took his hat off and said, "Mr. President, I would like to give you a present." I said, "That's very kind of you. What is it?" The rider said, "It's a bag of dog food, Mr. President." I answered, "That's very nice, but I do not have a dog here." The rider said, "Oh excuse me, Mr. President, but I thought that every blind man has a dog" (judge's joke!).

Once when I was judging at the Trojan Horse Trials in Arizona, there was a young rider's division. A young rider had a terrible test. When he saluted at the end of his dressage, he said, "Mr. President, I would like to apologize for this pornographic ride." And that is true. I ended up using that expression quite a bit afterward during some pretty terrible tests.

THANK YOU, SUSAN!

While judging the Three-Day Event at the Atlanta Olympics, we judges had a very hard time of it. We were judging two events: the individual and the team competitions, which overlapped for part of it. The first week was very badly organized. We had to wait in line for our food with the volunteers and with a very limited amount of time to eat. We had no vehicle, and Susan had to drive the whole Ground Jury from the hotel to the showground each day. The hotel had no bar and no restaurant, and there were no arrangements for us to eat there. Thanks go to Susan, who organized our dinner reservations every night as well as a short cocktail hour in our hotel room. Without her, I don't know what we would have done. Thank you, Susan, thank you, Susan, thank you, Susan!

Susan went to the FEI and the second week was greatly improved when her efforts gained us access to the FEI tent. It was not so fortunate for the athletes. Some athletes missed their competitions because the bus drivers were military personnel who had no knowledge of where to go for the events. It was surprising after the very successful 1984 Olympics in Los Angeles.

One time I was in England judging a CCI and went with the Ground Jury to dinner. In the same restaurant were some riders from different nations, having a great time. They were singing some Ray Charles songs, and so forth. The following morning, before the horse inspection, as President of the Ground Jury I came dressed up with a pair of very thick sunglasses and a white cane and a dog and walked up and down the jogging strip. I think the riders got the idea. It started the day with a joyful note because I am one who believes that you have to be very serious when you work, as long as you don't take yourself too seriously when you're not officiating!

17

THE FEI THREE-DAY EVENTING COMMITTEE

The FEI Three-Day Eventing Committee is made up of the chair, a rider representative, an organizer representative and three elected members representing individual zones. The FEI's aim is to have a judge and a technical delegate on the committee so that every aspect of the sport is represented and it was as a judge that I was elected in 1999.

Because of my background, I was given some specific tasks during my four-year tenure on the committee from 1999 to 2003. One was approving the new CCI dressage tests written by the British rider Christopher Bartle. Chris had ridden at the international level in both eventing and dressage and was more than equipped for this job. Because of the evolution of the CICs and the desire not to have the horses and riders performing the same dressage test over and over again I was asked to write tests for the CIC*/**/***, one new test for each level that would add to the existing ones. I also worked closely with Chris to ensure that these tests led the horses through a logical progression into the tests he was writing for the CCIs.

Another task was to develop an Eventing World Cup competition along the lines of the already established dressage, driving, and show-jumping World Cups. What I had to do was create special rules and regulations for the World Cup event based on the CIC*** level, which was the highest level at the time. The purpose of the World Cup was to promote the sport throughout the world, making it accessible to countries that did not have the riders, the horses, the organization or the means to have a CCI schedule on their own. Each country could have one qualifying competition at the *** level. Some countries like the United States, England, and Australia that had a lot of riders could have more than one qualifier if they applied for it and World Cup committee agreed.

I started to work on it in 2000, and it took about two years to put all the rules and regulations together. Although it was to be at the CIC*** level, the rules could be adapted to make the World Cup qualifiers and final "special." For instance, the rules allowed for flexibility, such as higher and wider jumps during the show jumping phase. Everyone realized that it was a good idea to have a bigger show jumping course, and as a result, this approach came into use across the board at all FEI-level competitions.

Each country was allowed to enter a specific number riders in the final according to their standings in the eventing world. The top countries got to send three or four riders, the next group two or three riders, and so on. I wanted to have about 40 to 45 riders in the final.

At first, I was looking for a general sponsor to sponsor the qualifiers and World Cup worldwide. I soon realized that it was more wishful thinking than a real possibility. So, my thinking switched to having each organizer of a qualifier, as well as the final, find their own sponsor. It was the only way that the World Cup could fly. The rules suggested that each sponsor would provide $30,000 in prize money for a qualifier and $80,000 to $100,000 in prize money for the final. I used the word "suggested" because organizers in smaller or developing countries might not necessarily be able to raise that kind of prize money.

Passing on the Baby

The first World Cup Eventing final took place in Pau, France, in 2003. It went very well. The whole idea was very well received, and it worked. This competition was the last event I judged and was my last assignment as an FEI judge. Since my Three-Day Event Committee term was now over, it was time to pass on the World Cup to someone else. The diapers were clean, and I was ready to pass on the baby. So, I gave the World Cup up to the FEI, and they said they would take it from there.

I hoped that the World Cup would end up becoming what it was created for and with the same level of importance as the World Cup competitions in other disciplines.

The World Cup formula came to serve another very useful purpose. Following the Sydney Olympics, and completely out of the blue, it came to the eventing world's notice that our sport was in danger of being dropped from the Olympic Games. During the 2002 Equestrian World Games in Jerez de la Frontera, Spain, FEI President Donar Pilar de Bourbon called a meeting of the FEI Three-Day Eventing Committee to address this issue. Some individuals had already made some protests privately, which were not necessarily the best way to handle the situation. At the meeting, Doña Pilar informed us that she had a plan to deal with this delicate subject. She wanted all private initiatives to stop for the moment. Her plan was to suggest the World Cup formula as the answer. It was a very lucky coincidence that the World Cup formula was ready, and it did, in fact, provide solutions to the major arguments that the International Olympic Committee (IOC) invoked to put the three-day event out of the Olympic program, namely:

1. It was often difficult to find the amount of land necessary to stage a full CCI in a geographically acceptable radius of the Olympic venue.

2. The expenses were very high when it came to preparing a suitable site for the cross-country, roads and tracks and stee-

plechase. Olympic organizers often had to create new dressage and show jumping facilities just for the Three Day Event as the pure dressage and show jumping facilities were often too far away from the cross-country site to serve a double purpose.

3.   There were too few nations that could produce teams if the CCI qualifying requirement was adhered to.

Obviously, the World Cup CIC formula satisfied most of the arguments posed by the IOC. Donar Pilar, through her diplomatic contacts and her determination, was able to save the day and keep eventing in the Olympics by proposing the World Cup CIC format and convincing the IOC that it was a satisfactory alternative.

Let me say here and now, no opportunity was given to us to save the original long format used in every Olympic Games since 1912. If we had insisted on keeping that formula, eventing would have been over as an Olympic sport. The message quite categorically was: "Change it or it is out!" We had to find an alternative, and that was that.

Also, it was made clear to us by the IOC that the individual and team competitions that had been in place since Atlanta would have to go. The two separate competitions had been devised in response to the IOC's argument that two medals could not be awarded for one competitive effort. In all Olympic Games up to and including Barcelona in 1992, a single competition was held and out of that one competition, the top three teams and top three individuals were awarded medals for this one effort. In Atlanta and Sydney, the team competition took place separately from the individual competition. While this system addressed the IOC's concern and allowed more horses and riders to participate, there is no doubt that it also created a significant additional expense for the organizing committees of those Games.

A way to solve this dilemma had to be found. How do you reward both the team and the individual when you can only run one horse one time? The FEI Three-Day Committee proposed that the team competition would run as normal and then the top 25 horses and riders would come back later in the day to jump an additional show-jumping round. The scores would be cumulative and the top three riders after the second round of show jumping would take the individual medals. This proposal would have resulted in unacceptable stress on the horses if the longer CCI format remained in place.

The IOC accepted this proposal and decided to put it into effect in Beijing in 2008. As it turned out, the Athens Olympic Organizing Committee was under immense pressure both from a financial standpoint and from a timing standpoint and petitioned to use the new formula in 2004. The IOC accepted its petition.

I personally believed and was quoted in a number of articles stating that the traditional CCI format should stay at the larger events; there is room for both, and there should be a circuit of CCI's with a championship as an end goal. Others, particularly in Europe, said that the move should be completely toward the CIC or the new Olympic format. The result of that viewpoint was totally unexpected. The speed with which Europe adopted the short format was cataclysmic for traditionalists who believe that the long format is the sport at its finest and who are adamantly opposed to changing it. First, the organizers of the 2006 World Equestrian Games in Aachen applied to run in the short format. Next, the various European CCI's elected to run the short format and in the most surprising move, at least to me, the "big ones" Badminton and Burghley announced that they would move to the short format in 2006. The Rolex Kentucky Three-day Event was the last classic four-star three-day event on the calendar. As reluctant as they were, if Rolex organizers Janie Atkinson and Equestrian Events Inc. wanted to continue as a selection trial preparing horses for Olympic and World Championship Teams, they would have to acquiesce and transition to the short format.

FLEXIBILITY HAS A PLACE

There had been a need for a more flexible shorter format for some time. At Lexington some years before, I conducted, as the coach, an experiment on a shorter format out of necessity. My reasoning was that I wanted the horses tested on the crucial phases of the endurance day without having to bring them to their peak of performance before the next upcoming major championship. The date of the championship was just too soon after Lexington to allow the horses to compete in a full phase three-day event and then allow time for them to have their necessary break before getting them fit again to participate in the big one. I tried this experiment two years in a row for this reason. The model I used was to run a steeplechase phase before the cross-country, but I eliminated Phases A and C, the roads and tracks.

I had a hard time believing that Phase A was the ideal warm-up for the steeplechase. I have ridden races over jumps, and I never did a Phase A for a warm-up. I had an even harder time believing that Phase C is a recuperative phase before the cross-country. So, I had the riders warm up their horses as they wished for the steeplechase, and when they finished that phase they walked their horses to the start of cross-country and warmed up for the cross-country again as they pleased. The time between the steeplechase and the cross-country was about 50 minutes, roughly the time normally allowed on Phase C.

The statistics taken at Lexington during those two experimental years were very clear. The horses were without a doubt in much better shape to start on cross-country than they were when they had had to do a Phase C roads and tracks.

For me, the dream format would be to have a steeplechase to test the ability of the horse to jump at speed and then do the cross-country. But I know that it is not a practical thing to organize, and it is not often that you can have a good steeplechase course in proximity to the cross-country start.

This approach would be my ideal because it would test the horses' quality and would favor the Thoroughbred types, which are my favorite (likely because of my racing background). On the other hand, I believed with the new formula that if the cross-country course is well conceived, horses will still need to gallop to come within the time. So, I hoped, we would not have half-bred horses becoming stars.

I do want to say that I do not believe it is the speed that is hard on event horses. Racehorses run 10 to 20 races a year putting out a much more violent effort. Likewise, it is not the endurance that is hard on them. What is hard is the combination of both: speed *and* endurance, which is the term used to describe the CCI long format. If you can run your horse twice a year in the classic CCI format, you should be happy, and you are lucky, but you would not want to run him in more than that. So in my mind the CIC and the CCI can coexist for the benefit of the horses, riders, owners, sponsors, and organizers.

While it is sad to see the end of the sport as we have known it all of these years and indeed, all of my lifetime, it must be said that the sport has to evolve into something that is marketable and profitable if it is to survive at all. We just have to make the best of it as it is today. So, short of realizing my dream format, I would have liked to see the classic CCI long format remain at the four-star level as well as the two-star level for Young Riders. However, the FEI stated that all of its championships would run in the short format, that is, without a steeplechase. So, the traditional three-day event is a thing of the past for all international championships.

Whether long format or short format, the best riders from years ago would be among the best today because they were the best then at the game they were playing. The same applies the other way around. The top-class riders of today would be among the best back then. Furthermore, regardless of which format they would still excel because that is the nature of those riders—they would be winners no matter when, no matter what. The same riders that won the old classic three-days are still winning the short-format events.

In fact, it is the riders who will decide what the sport will be and where it is going. An organizer needs good quality horses and riders to participate in large enough numbers to justify their efforts in producing a good show, and I think that is exactly the way it should be. At the end of the day, it is the riders who make the show. And, it will be the riders who decide the sport's future.

Many people have said that this is not in the tradition of the military that gave birth to eventing. I say, we are no longer in the military, there is no cavalry anymore, and we have to evolve. A word of caution: if we start to see shorter courses with more jumps coming at the horses faster, we will see problems. Horses cannot keep up with that number of jumps coming that quickly. Their brains just cannot cope. We must be careful that as we cater to the spectator by building courses with fences closer together so that they can all be seen from one spot, we keep in mind that the horse has not changed, and is not changing regarding its physical and mental capacity. It is possible that in order to create a sport that satisfies the spectators' needs we create one that the horse can no longer do. The horse does not walk the course; he has not seen the fences he will be asked to jump, the terrain to be negotiated, and the questions he will have to answer. His reflexes will be put to the test one jump after another, faster and faster and after a while, he will no longer know what he is doing. Horses are the way they are, and their reactions are not changing. You can only ask just so much of their reflexes. The cross-country needs to have some length to it. A solution would be to have several fences in close proximity so that the public are entertained and then have a galloping stretch over easier fences to the next complex of fences. The speeds should not be reduced. If there are adverse weather conditions, then shorten the course by all means, but the speed should be left alone. The height of the fences is not really a problem. I have always said that you can build a cross-country course of three-foot jumps that is completely un-jumpable!

All of that being said, I have a great deal of sympathy for course designers who have the difficult task of separating the very best from the very good by asking the right questions. Today's horses are of such quality and experience that it is very hard to get the right balance of difficulty without creating something that only two or three horses in the world can complete.

One aspect that course designers have to guard against is unreasonable competition between each other. There has been a tendency to try and outdo the previous course designer on a particular site by creating something bigger, fancier, and more expensive. No one likes to admit it, but it is a valid point and leads to impossible questions being asked, as well as costing an exorbitant amount to build.

It is also my belief that there are 15 to 20 top riders in the world at any one time. There are another 30 to 40 legitimate international riders and in my opinion, the rest do not belong at the four-star level. This is why we have seen some of the dreadful and fatal accidents in the sport. We not only have to look at the technical difficulty of today's courses but we also have to look at the rules and how changes to them might affect the sport. In the late 1990s we changed the penalties on the cross-country to one for each second over the optimum time, two-and-a-half times the penalties as before. Riders did not ride the course according to their their abilities and that of their horses but went for speed and accidents happened. In one season we had more than a dozen fatalities worldwide. The deaths that occurred during 1997 to 1999 caused us to reevaluate everything about the sport and in particular the nature of the falls and the specific fences involved. We saw how horses were rotating as they fell over the fences and as a result landing on the riders. Some of that is sheer bad luck, and you will never be able to take the element of risk out of the sport. However, things can be done to reduce the possibility of this type of rotational fall. We have changed the way fences are designed; we have changed the flow of the courses to eliminate some obvious dangers. One of these is the siting of the alternative routes on fences and the introduction of black flag options. For instance, courses used to allow for the rider to make split second decisions when a horse refused at the straight route. Often the rider could turn the horse immediately to the right or left and jump a wing of the fence that formed the alternative route and, thereby, save precious seconds. This frequently had the effect of asking the horse to jump if not from a standstill then from a very close distance at a very slow pace. Horses were in danger of catching a leg and somersaulting over the fence landing on the rider. A crushing fall of this nature can be fatal. We changed the rules immediately to prevent that. Now there are no such time-saving temptations. If a rider needs to jump the alternative route he has to go considerably out of his way to regroup and jump a separate fence. The FEI put together a task force under Britain's Lord Hartington to look into improving all aspects of safety. The Task Force included Jackie Stewart, a former Formula One motor racing champion who had worked tirelessly to improve safety standards in auto racing, and other notable experts including David O'Connor. The group produced a comprehensive report on safety, and we have seen many new initiatives implemented as a result of their work.

The art of course design has come a long way, but it seems we have gone from one extreme to another. The cross-country course at the Stockholm Olympics in 1956 is an example of one extreme in course building and the course at the World Equestrian Games in Jerez with its many options was at the other end of the spectrum. Stockholm was very rustic with natural looking obstacles, somewhat flimsy, and built over whatever terrain was there. Jerez was beautifully built with elaborate jump complexes that had been treated to some fancy carpentry work. Also, the number of options offered must have increased their construction costs substantially.

Today we have courses with fences looking like they came straight out of the furniture store. They are run over footing that resembles a putting green on a golf course. While I am adamant that the footing should be good and the course creative and visually attractive, I think we can go too far in our demands and all of that puts an enormous financial burden on the organizers. Perhaps there is some middle ground where the technical complexes are designed with a theme and situated around a course of big, natural hedges, with ditches and banks made of whatever materials are available locally. The aim should be to require forward riding. We cannot allow the commercial aspect to change the sport to the detriment of the horses and riders as well as the financial ruin of the organizers.

I proposed to the FEI that a list be created of trained and qualified horsemen to serve as course inspectors to any organizer of any championship. One month before the competition, these inspectors would visit the site with the designer and the technical delegate to give it the seal of approval. The Ground Jury should not have to make any changes when they arrive at the competition (other than those required by adverse weather conditions) because by that time it is too late to make any major adjustments. This proposal was adopted and is now in use.

I have ruffled some feathers over the years, but I sincerely love eventing and as I have said, this is not a popularity contest, so I have no trouble speaking my mind. Again, the sport is a wonderful thing to behold when it is done right and it is a disaster when it is not. Let no one be in doubt—eventing does not tolerate mediocrity.

PART IV

THE LE GOFF PHILOSOPHY

"Riding is like religion—you've GOT to believe!

18

ON DRESSAGE

Today, dressage is not only the primary essential element for training horses in all aspects of eventing, cross-country, and show jumping, but it has become a "must" if you are to figure in the top placings at the end of the competition. There was a time when you could be in the middle of the pack after dressage and still win. That is history. In the last few years, especially since the middle 1990s, the quality of the dressage performances has increased significantly. The caliber of today's top horses is astonishing, and the riding has also become something that is enjoyable to watch, it is so good.

The remarkable thing is that now you are unable to tell from what nationality the rider is unless you look at the saddle pad. Of course, not all riders are in that league, but if you go to a top class international event and let's say there are 80 starters, 10 of them are likely to be the group from which the first three finishers will come.

Many competitors now go clear cross-country jumping and within the time, and they also manage to get a clear round on the show-jumping phase, so it is evident that the dressage is what makes the difference in the top placings. In other words, you win it in dressage and lose it afterward.

There has been a lot of splendid literature on dressage by very qualified and talented authors on the subject, so my purpose here is not to write another one. Rather, I want to make some points and suggestions that will hopefully motivate the reader to move the intellect from the seat, where the intelligence of many riders resides, up to the brain.

Today, the world of dressage is much more unified in its style than it has ever been before, and this includes pure dressage. That unified style is due to a number of factors. First, there are a lot more international competitions where riders and trainers have many opportunities to observe each other. Second, particularly in pure dressage, the type of horses we are seeing is more consistent. Third, modern technology and the availability of videos and DVDs has had a distinct impact on bringing the type of horses, the way of riding them, and the training methods used much closer together.

THE RIDING SCHOOLS TRADITION AND THE TYPE OF HORSES USED

The tradition of the French School at Saumur, where I trained, developed over a couple of centuries and was different from the Spanish Riding School in Vienna. Saumur practiced high school dressage as well as *sauteurs*, or "airs above the ground." *Sauteurs* in Saumur also presented 12 horses at a time in a "ride" whereas at the Spanish Riding School there are a lot of individual demonstrations. Many of these are "in hand," meaning that instead of riding the horse the handler walks alongside and controls the horse from the reins in his hands. Saumur's philosophy is that when trained correctly, all breeds can perform together. The Spanish Riding School uses only Lipizzaners. The school of Jerez, in Spain, also concentrates on one breed, the Andalusian.

Saumur also teaches and prepares the military for riding horses into battle. This led the Cadre Noir to practice all of the disciplines; show jumping, dressage, eventing, and racing were all part of the training of the horses, and it led to better cavalry riders. Riding in dressage quadrilles as well as the *sauteurs* was highly intensive training.

James Fillis (1834–1913) was a disciple of the French School and as a consequence and due to his expertise he was well suited to accept the invitation of the Grand Duke Nicholas to train the Russian Cavalry. The Russian Cavalry was using Anglo-Arabs horses with a lot of Thoroughbred blood, and they rode these with considerable success due to his influence.

All three schools study dressage in its highest form. However, the high school quadrille in Saumur is much more the type of high school dressage found in a Grand Prix test in international competition today. The riding masters in Vienna worked on the principle of François Robichon de La Guérinière (1688–1751). His principles of dressage are still very much in favor with the Spanish Riding School in Vienna who find it suits their Lipizzaner horses. Over the years they have done a superb job of ensuring the Lipizzaner's survival. They put on extremely professional demonstrations, which have today become popular entertainment.

Because I am French, it was my ambition to become a member of the Cadre Noir. It not only practices the high school movements and the *sauteurs*, it also allows and even encourages you to practice and take part in racing, eventing, steeplechasing, and show jumping. It did, and does today, focus on the more modern style of dressage in the high school manner. Because Saumur is not breed-specific, the school can produce horses for all types of competition: eventing, show jumping, driving, vaulting, all the disciplines that fall under the FEI umbrella, plus steeplechasing. The dressage or high school quadrille and the *sauteur* quadrille, which is the essence of the Cadre Noir, are composed of many different breeds of horses, for example, Thoroughbred, Anglo-Arab, Selle Français, and other breeds. The philosophy being that if the different horses are trained the same way, they should be able to perform together in the quadrille.

One of my dearest friends and a former pupil, Jacques Remiat, a riding master who has now retired from the Cadre Noir, is a classic example of the multi-faceted and diverse horsemen produced by Saumur. He had two horses, one of which he competed in Grand Prix dressage and steeplechase races. The same horse and the same rider! He had another horse that did the dressage quadrille in the high school and competed with him in eventing and show jumping at the same time. Jacques' horse often performed in the high school quadrille followed a week later by an event followed by a show-jumping competition the next week, all of which demonstrates the Cadre Noir's philosophy of teaching all-around horsemanship. The top class riders in the old days were trained to do all these disciplines. My father taught all his show jumpers to passage and piaffe, and I used to jump some pretty good-sized fences out of passage (for fun). Not only are the riders able to do it but the horses can do it. Today you might see an event horse retire from eventing and go on to train and compete in dressage, but not compete in both at the same time.

Remarkably, with a few exceptions today, the top class dressage horses look very much alike regardless of which nation they represent. Germany, Holland, Denmark, and several other countries are breeding quality horses with much more noble blood than was done before World War II and these horses are much more readily available today "for a price."

As far as dressage in eventing is concerned, there is still some diversity in the horses reaching the top, but my God, do we see some beautiful animals, free movers, flowing and with a lot of expression. I could say that some of them give me a lot of "emotion" during their dressage test.

THE BASICS OF DRESSAGE
What is riding all about?

- Going forward.

- Coming back.

- Turning.

Good dressage should make these three facts easier and easier as your training progresses. Accepted principles in achieving these goals should be respected. They are a guideline to which riders should refer, especially when the schooling does not progress well. The accepted principles are:

- Forward.

- Calm.

- Straight.

If you want to get more detailed, you should concentrate on understanding the progression of dressage, using the Training Pyramid in building up the education of the horse. That is now more of a method rather than principles. The Pyramid is:

1. Paces, rhythm, regularity.

2. Relaxation and suppleness, both physical and mental.

3. Acceptance of the bridle.

4. "Impulsion," the desire to move forward while staying balanced.

5. "Straightness," equal bending of the whole longitudinal axis of the horse.

6. Engagement of the hindquarters, which allows free motion depending on the difficulty of the movement.

These are the principles and the method that should be used in training and progression for every sport horse.

Dressage is a lot simpler than some people would like to make it. The first thing to do is to learn how to ride properly. The better you ride, the easier it is going to be to train horses, and a good event rider should be one who can ride and be comfortable at a Prix St. George level and above. He is one who should ride steeplechase races to develop the feel of rhythm, speed, and balance. He is one who should ride show jumping at a much higher level than eventing requires—that is, be comfortable in the show ring the last day at the event, as a rail down can make a huge difference in the final placings.

Dressage comes from the French, and it means schooling and training. For instance, a French person would say, "I am sending my bird dog to a trainer for dressage." The word is not purely the prerogative of the horse world. Behind the word "dressage" is a whole world of making the horse much more rideable in the different disciplines of equestrian sports.

To practice and produce good dressage there are three essential things:

- First is to have a good seat.

- Second is to have a good seat.

- Third is to have a good seat.

It is a necessary condition to be comfortable on a horse as this will make you more accurate with your aids and assist in communication with your horse. A rider has to acquire complete control of his or her body to be in harmony with the horse. Seat muscles should be relaxed, as opposed to tennis balls, to make you sit in the saddle. The lower back should be very supple because it is the liaison between what belongs to the body of the horse which is the part of the rider below the belt, that is, the hips, the seat, and the legs. The upper body above the belt, which includes the shoulders, arms, elbows, wrists, hands and head, belongs to the mouth of the horse with the reins being only the continuation of the rider's arms.

Today, many people learn to compete before they learn how to ride, and that makes it difficult for them to be truly competitive and to progress successfully to the other levels, so is that not "defeating the purpose?" Time spent in the school perfecting your art is never wasted.

All of that should work to produce a good position. Position is form and form is function. I clearly remember a conversation I had with Lucinda Green back in the 70s in Hamilton, Massachusetts. She was in the United States for a visit and was unable to fly home as scheduled. I was conducting a training session with the US Team and Lucinda asked me if I had a horse for her to ride in the session.

After she had ridden, Lucinda said she realized she did not have enough basic training, and she had already won Badminton! Apparently, she worked on her training and did whatever it took to correct it and became the very successful rider she was, winning Badminton a total of six times.

There is no doubt in my mind that even in our modern days of technology, the longe line, and the work without stirrups on the flat and up and down hills is the best way to acquire a good seat. A good seat is the key element essential to the schooling and production of a good dressage horse. Without a good seat, your aids cannot be precise and accurate as you are not in perfect control of your body motions. A good seat allows the rider to be precise with his natural aids, hands, legs, and weight. When witnessing a very good dressage test, concentrate for a moment on the rider. You will undoubtedly realize that she has not only a good position but also has definite control of her body motions, which allow her to be in harmony with her horse and to show her full potential in the dressage ring. The position is what you have to strive to acquire first because position = form and form = function.

Clinics are useful, mainly for the educated riders, but unfortunately these days, clinicians teach cross-country and show jumping but very few teach dressage. There is not one way to ride in dressage and another way to ride cross-country and still another way to ride show jumping. It is all the same technique. Go forward, come back, and turn, and a well-trained horse does that very smoothly.

Take the canter work as an example. Say you are working with an average-size horse of 16.0 to 16.2 hands. Obviously, the type and conformation of the event horse is different from the pure dressage horse, but he still has to be trained and judged using the same criteria. Experiment with counting the strides between two letters at the ends of the long side of a 60-meter dressage ring. At the working canter you will have 16 strides, at a medium canter 14 strides, at a collected canter you could get up to 20 strides, and at an extended canter you could possibly get 12 strides. When the dressage test asks for collected and extended canter that is what it means—the lengths of the stride, of course. Now think what you can do with a horse that truly does the above. You can use it for jumping, shortening and lengthening the stride, and to adjust the distance between fences; this is what dressage is all about and what it *should* be all about.

Of course, if you look at a pure dressage horse versus an event horse, the picture is different. One has to do only dressage, and the other has to run and jump out in the country and then show jump in an enclosed arena. Obviously, dressage horses that are pretty stereotyped today are much shorter-coupled with an elevated neck versus an event horse that is called upon to run and jump, so his confirmation is closer to a racehorse or steeplechaser. The overall picture is noticeably different.

One of the most challenging questions ever asked of me came from a reporter at a competition. He said, "Sir, I do not know anything about horses, and in watching the rider doing his ride (he meant the dressage test) I was wondering how does the rider tell the horse what to do?"

Well, I was standing in front of this gentleman and honestly did not know how to answer him in a few words. "You see it is a bit complicated to explain," I said. "It would almost take a book to answer your question."

Obviously, I was not satisfied with my answer, and as I often do in these cases where I need to think about something I take my fishing rod and go and hide somewhere. And in a lot of cases, I find my answer when coming back from my escapade. So off I went.

As I sat on the bank of the river, I asked myself this question, "Assuming that I want a canter depart from my horse, what happens?" First, it is my brain that tells my body (natural aids) to physically put my legs, weight, and hands in the specific places where I have been taught to put them to ask for a canter depart.

Second, the horse registers my request in his brain, and as he has been trained to, he feels my aids, legs, seat, and hands in the correct places for a canter depart. Having registered this command, his brain then tells his body to respond accordingly. In other words, there is a simple chain of communication between the horse and the rider that works this way:

1. Your brain to your body.

2. Your body to the horse's brain using physical contact—the aids.

3. His brain processes your aids and sends the message to his body.

It is very simple and very logical, and that is what I should have said to the reporter. I do not know about you, but I have never read this in any book. I do know though my students are using it and I am glad because there is no mystery in dressage.

Of course, the more experienced the horse becomes the shorter the time the cycle takes. For example, look at a horse in a show-jumping jump off, and watch his eyes. You can see exactly at what moment the horse sees the fence that he is supposed to jump. The rider knows when he wants to turn and through his body position and balance tells the horse where to go. The horse registers this very quickly in his brain and reads the jump. The cycle of rider's brain to rider's body to horse's brain to horse's body has been accomplished, and it happened very quickly because the horse is so well trained and experienced.

Most of the time when you have a wrong canter depart, it is because you have not allowed the cycle to take place, or your body communication with your horse is not clear enough.

OBEDIENCE...NOT SLAVERY

We have all lost our temper at times when working with horses. Again, most of the time it is because the channel of communication does not work; the horse does not understand what we want from him, and we get mad. Well, it is always our mistake. When you are about to get mad at your horse think that if you are rude to a person, you can always go and apologize, but you cannot apologize to horses! And if they do not have what we call intelligence, they for sure have a great memory, and it takes a long time to erase a bad riding session with your horse. It is too bad that when you fully understand these things you may be too old to put them to work so I guess all you can do is tell your experiences to others, hoping that some people will believe you and benefit from the telling.

I also believe that we do not pay enough attention to understanding how our horses think. If you want to become a genuinely good horse person, you have to learn to think like a horse because you cannot make the horse think like you!

Modern life has not always served our friends the horses well. We tend to use them to satisfy our goals. Many competition horses, particularly dressage horses and some show horses, go from their stall to the ring and the ring to the stall. Some never get to be turned out for different reasons be it lack of available paddocks or an even more shameful one: they are worth so much money that the rider cannot allow them to get hurt in a pasture. The so-called show hunter becomes a far cry from the field hunter that he is supposed to represent at his best.

Having been to so many Olympic Games and many other top horse competitions, I always make a point of going to see the schooling of the pure dressage riders after the eventing competition is over. At Montreal in 1976, I saw the horse that eventually won running away out of the schooling ring totally out of control. I felt he had had enough. Seeing him win the individual gold medal a few days later troubled me.

In Sydney, I witnessed a top class rider with a beautiful horse work him nonstop with no break for way over one hour. The horse was sweating heavily and very tense. Maybe he just needed to take a pee but was not given the chance. Just imagine how you would feel if someone kept after you and you could not get to go....

Again experience and observation teach you these things, like schooling a horse before the competition and then allowing time to take him to his stall for a few moments where he can relieve himself. Some horses will not do this while they are mounted.

So never confuse submission and obedience with slavery. If you are a very experienced and powerful rider, you will be able to force your horse to perform up to the point where you will have to rely on him to do things for you. If he trusts you and wants to please you, he will try his very best. But if he does not like you, he might just set you on the wrong side of the jump.

TO THE TECHNICAL

After these somewhat philosophical remarks, let's talk about more technical points. Regarding the different movements required in a dressage test, each is clearly described, and the way they should be performed is outlined in the USEF Rule Book and most other international rule books.

The best way to learn the tests themselves and the geometry of the different movements is to draw them on draft paper. It is very easy to make blanks of a dressage court to scale, and go to a copy machine and make as many blanks as you need. You can then draw your dressage tests to scale. Drawing the dressage figures will help you to understand the design, geometry, and the accuracy of each of the different movements.

The English language does not make it easy to explain the different stages of "on the bit." But I will try to explain the French definitions.

First, *sur la main* literally means on your hand, meaning that the horse accepts the bit in his mouth and accepts the contact through the reins with the rider's hands.

Second, *placer* means that the horse, in addition to accepting the bit in his mouth and the contact with the rider's hand, is flexed at the end of the neck. The front of his head is close to the vertical, but the neck is not collected and remains out in front of the rider.

Third, *le ramener* is the next important stage. The forehead of the horse remains close to the vertical, but the neck is more elevated and collected. The rider produces this by increasing the impulsion, creating the energy needed to go forward, and then limiting the forward motion using the reins. In simple terms, since the energy or so-called impulsion is not allowed to be used completely in going forward, it has to go somewhere and that is what helps to shorten and elevate the neck, mainly the base of the neck. The poll should remain the highest point of the neck.

Now our horse is "in hand" and collected in front. Obviously, the energy, or impulsion, is created by the rider's legs, and it is the hindquarters, the engine of the horse, that pushes forward. When somewhat contained in the rider's hands this puts him in the *ramener*.

Fourth, *le rassembler* is the last stage in classical high school, where the horse is in the *ramener* elevation of the forehand with the engagement and impulsion necessary to teach the high school movements like piaffe, passage, tempi changes, and so on. That is the highest and final form of "on the bit," which is pretty much the only English expression to cover all the above stages. If you think about each step, you should comprehend that all this is to be achieved by pushing from back to front. At the second stage visualize a fencing athlete pushing his épée into the wall and taking little steps forward. The wall is the bit; the fencer is the horse's hindquarters, and the épée is the horse's neck and body. As the fencer progressively moves forward towards the wall, the épée bends upward accordingly. The mantra is back to front, back to front, always back to front. That is the opposite of bringing the horse's head back toward you with no engagement of the hindquarters and no impulsion. All those "contraceptives," as I call them, the draw-reins and other equipment, will produce false dressage and your horse will not be able to progress correctly as most of the time these "contraceptives" are used improperly.

I have talked about the front, now how about the hindquarters: *when you have the mouth you may have the haunches, but when you have the haunches you always have the mouth!* I leave it to your creative imagination to come up with some comparisons that can make you smile and possibly transport your mind to some pleasant memories.

To "control the haunches" starts with teaching horse (and rider) the art of leg-yielding where the horse must be moving willingly away from a predominant leg behind the girth along the wall or across the diagonal. When the horse becomes fluidly obedient to the leg in this manner, everything else becomes easy regarding all lateral work, shoulder-in, rein-back, half-pass, work around the haunches, and so on.

Now you have the control of the forehand and the control of the haunches and from there you can teach him whatever you want; he is yours.

Good luck with him!

19

ON CONDITIONING THE
EVENT HORSE

The mental attitude of the horse is of equal importance as the physical conditioning. A relaxed, happy horse will not only compete better but will have far less chance of injury. If a horse is happy in his work, then competing at an event will take less out of him. A calm horse has a longer stride. Take one extra foot on a stride, and multiply that by the number of strides on a cross-country course and you will see a big difference. The horse will be faster on the course with no increase in speed because he is taking fewer strides to do it. The development of your conditioning program should include both the body and the mind and will help the horse do his job at maximum efficiency.

Conversely, if the horse is unhappy, he may not make the extra effort. You can pretty much get the horse up to the Preliminary level whether he enjoys it or not. But when it comes to the big fences, you cannot force him. It is all down to the mental attitude; many horses are physically capable of jumping the heights and widths, but they just will not do it. Horses have to like you and be happy in their work to put out that kind of effort. I see some people who do not ride so well, but horses go for them. I believe someone like that must be a good horseman or horsewoman because the horse wants to work for him or her.

Injuries are often related to the horse's mental condition. If a horse is relaxed, he is not going to get into half the trouble he will if he is fighting the rider all through the course. Not only is the unhappy horse going to knock himself, he is also going to have problems in his back, muscle soreness, and problems in the shoulders, all because he is mentally unhappy and tense. He is going to run around with his head in the air, unresponsive to his rider, who will then head to the hardware store for a solution instead of the drawing board!

The happy horse will use his body properly. He will be able to make the time between jumps; he will seem like he is flowing, coming back smoothly for turns and flowing forward. His muscles will work freely. The tendons will slide inside the tendon sheath, and they will seldom be injured. The articulated joints will work fluidly. There will be no rubbing or grating because the horse is relaxed. His muscles are relaxed and he is supple, listening, obediently responding to the rider's aids, and he is covering the ground with relaxed, efficient strides, not wasting an ounce of his energy. This is the epitome of our goal in our training and conditioning program. And again, it all comes down to going forward, coming back, and turning smoothly like a well-oiled machine.

Although there are basic principles to conditioning horses, I never trained two teams the same way and have always adjusted the conditioning of event horses according to specific factors, such as:

1. The distances and speed required and the nature of the terrain of the target competition.

2. The length of time since the horse's last competition. A horse that has not been competing for several months will need more conditioning than one who is competing regularly.

3. The facilities available for conditioning. Gently rolling open fields are ideal, some hills would be an asset, but you must make the best of what you have nearby.

4. The temperament of the horse. With a hot horse, you must use a lot of long distances at slower speeds. With a more easygoing horse you will use shorter distances at faster speeds.

5. The age and soundness of the horse. With a horse whose soundness is delicate, you must replace the speed work on the flat with slower work uphill and possibly swimming.

6. The upcoming competitions. When conditioning for a three-day event, the horse trials leading up to it will be a critical part of the horse's fitness preparation and nothing can replace competition.

7. The rule of three. Three weeks prior to a major competition I always sharpen up the horses with a competition. If you have to travel a long distance to the final competition, then the trial can move to four weeks prior. Racehorse trainers would not conceive running the Kentucky Derby without prep races.

First, let me say that it is essential that a horse get a rest period after a hard season. They should be turned out for 10 hours a day in a safe pasture whenever possible and for at least three weeks. Young horses at the Preliminary and Intermediate levels don't need any riding during this decompression period, but an older horse may need a gentle hack to keep his joints loose and his back muscles in decent shape. A rest of less than three weeks simply will not do. Also, a midseason break just doesn't work as the horse simply won't let down during that short length of time, but you can give him what I call an "active rest." This means taking him for hacks with no work as such. It is better to let the groom do it if possible as you would be tempted to do something instead of leaving him alone. Horses can go sour more quickly than people. Treat them like people because they think and react to their conditions and they have feelings; they also need a vacation!

COMING BACK AFTER A LAYOFF

Now, let's consider a horse that has had more than two months off. The first step for any level of upcoming competition is to assure that your horse is a candidate for conditioning, that is when he is starting out healthy. A checkup is imperative and should include a blood count, dental work, and a manure check for any undigested grain as well as parasites. Your horse must be able to digest his food properly to gain the energy needed for the upcoming work. His lungs and heart must be fully functional; his legs must be pain-free. Have the farrier check his feet and get him on a good worming program. Have his teeth checked and floated. Look at your horse; see through the salon-like equine beauty products. Is his coat gleaming from his inner well-being, or is it out of a bottle?

Conditioning can be separated into two stages: a four-week legging-up period and then the galloping program. The latter is dependent upon the former, which begins gradually. Many riders are under the impression that pasture play keeps horses in good physical condition. However, this activity does not prepare your horse at all for carrying the weight of the rider.

During the initial legging-up phase, the horse's back must have a chance to get back in shape. Start by riding him out at the walk and alternate every other day with longeing. Either session should last about 20 minutes. The longeing should be done with a saddle and should include trot sessions of two to three minutes. Again, all ridden work will be limited to the walk.

Is he happy and enjoying his work? Palpate the muscles on either side of the spine on a daily basis to detect soreness. If there is tenderness in this region, you will feel and see him flinch when you apply some pressure. If this occurs, then cut back on the program until it is resolved. Just think for a moment about how your muscles feel when you begin a new exercise program, and you will understand how your horse feels!

After two weeks of alternate longeing and riding at the walk, your horse should be able to work under saddle six days a week. You may now start short trotting periods of three to four minutes. Gradually increase the number of trotting periods to about four or five four-minute sessions by the end of the fourth week. At this point, the horse is ready to begin a light training program.

During the four-week legging-up phase, there should be no formal training work in either dressage or jumping. The horse does not have the base of conditioning to either practice or improve. The purpose of the legging-up phase is to harden the tendons of the leg and condition the carrying muscles of the neck and spine. Most of this work should be done outside on the roads or trails. Remember: a three-day horse is not trained in an indoor arena!

The horse can now be introduced to training in dressage and jumping. Here are two typical schedules that might work for you.

The Younger or Greener Event Horse
Monday: Hack outside and dressage

Tuesday: Schooling over jumps

Wednesday: Dressage

Thursday: Schooling over jumps

Friday: Dressage

Saturday Gallop

Sunday: Day off

The Experienced Event Horse
Monday: Hack outside and dressage

Tuesday: Gallop

Wednesday: Dressage

Thursday: Schooling over jumps

Friday: Dressage

Saturday: Gallop

Sunday: Day off

Hacking out to warm up before the session or cool down after it will help keep the horse healthy in his mind. Do not pull him out of his stable, work him, then put him straight back in his stable so that you can work on the next horse. He *will* get stale and grumpy. Horses were not meant to stand in 12- by 12-foot box stalls all day. You must care about your horse because if you don't, he will not work for you.

Go with the Horse

Your horse determines the speed of the progress. Younger horses competing at lower levels will require less galloping (once per week), allowing more time for much-needed sessions of schooling over fences. An older, experienced horse will require less schooling over fences and will condition more slowly than his younger counterpart, which means he will benefit more from galloping twice a week. Every fifth day is a good guideline and not more often than every third day.

The next task is to develop a working, galloping pace that will serve as the basis for all further conditioning. Though the pace should approximate 375 to 400 meters per minute, the quality of the gait is paramount. It is not *what* you do but *how* you do it that counts. Two horses traveling at the same speed for the same distance are not necessarily working to the same degree. You must teach the horse to breathe with his stride, to balance his weight up and down hills, to lengthen and shorten his stride willingly, and to remain relaxed while concentrating. These skills minimize energy expenditure while increasing obedience. The result is maximum performance and minimal injury. You must learn to listen to the engine.

Mark off the perimeter of a field with meter markings that will help you develop a feel for the speed you are traveling. Memorize how it feels for your horse to go 400 meters per minute ("mpm"). You cannot rely on your watch alone.

Begin with a mile or a mile-and-a-half at this pace, then rest the horse and evaluate his level of energy. If it was easy for him then after a short (two to four minutes) period, do another gallop. Thus begins the interval training that will develop his heart and wind conditioning. The goal of interval training is to strengthen his heart muscle that pushes the blood more quickly, particular to his extremities, thus cleansing the lactic acid from his muscles. In interval training the periods of work become longer and the periods of rest become shorter as the horse grows fitter. The principle of interval training came from the lecture I attended in 1962 regarding track and field athletes, and I was the first one to use it in training event horses.

The length of the interval rest period is dependent on the horse as well as the outside temperature. Obviously, the horse recoups more quickly if it is not too hot or too cold. Strive to allow him to recover to one- to two-thirds of his working state and then resume. To do this, you must know beforehand your horse's resting rate and his maximum working rate. Proficiency at taking pulse and respiration are of obvious use in acquiring the ability to gauge the degree of recovery. You can ask your vet to give you a lesson in determining heart and respiratory rates.

For your basic conditioning, aim toward a total of double the distance required in the next competition. For example, in Preliminary cross-country courses, you will be galloping for two miles at 520 mpm. Intervals at the basic conditioning speed of 375 to 400 mpm should reach four miles of gallops. Once your horse is capable of this and is recovering well, the total distance can be decreased to approach actual competition course length at the required speed of the competition. For instance, your last work before competition could be two or three trot sets for five to 10 minutes as a warmup. Then do a one-mile gallop starting at 450 mpm and ending up at 500 mpm, a two-minute break, and another mile quickly up to 500 mpm and finishing at 550 to 600 mpm, using a slight hill if you can.

Again, measure your field with stakes, 500 meters, 600 meters, and so on, and time it so you know what that speed feels like. If needed, go to a racetrack.

Depending upon the length of the target competition, as the horse's condition improves you can increase the number of intervals (up to four), increase the distance (up to two miles), decrease the length of the rest period, and increase the speed over seven to eight weeks of galloping. Condition only as much as the test demands to keep your horse comfortable—no more.

Cross-country or steeplechase schooling should substitute for a gallop. If you do a strong gallop on Saturday, the horse should go out for a short session on Sunday to prevent muscles and tendons from shortening too much.

I like schooling my horses up and down hills with the same principles used in working on the flat in dressage. Too many people do dressage and then go out and gallop. The ring is not the only place that you do dressage. Do not ride one way in the ring and another way outside it. On the hills you can teach him to cadence his respiration. Keep bringing him back until he breathes with the stride. Teach him to lengthen and shorten while you are doing your hill work.

Teach him to balance himself going down hills. Tell him to "whoa" at the top and walk going down. He must walk down in a balanced manner with his legs under him. Condition by going faster up the hill and slower down the hill. Then when you are in competition you can let him go faster up a short hill and ask him to steady (or be consistent) up a long hill. If you know you have a steep downhill run to a jump, you can ask him to whoa at the top, and he will listen because he has been trained to do that. You can then go down the hill to the jump in a balanced way and will be able to go down faster than the other riders because you have trained your horse how to do it. You have schooled him while you were conditioning him, and he is engaged and balanced going down that hill, which makes him rideable to the jump.

INCORPORATING COMPETITION

As part of a conditioning program, a horse should compete in a few events in preparation for the three-day event. Even lower-level competitors can select a "goal competition" and schedule early events as part of their program. Actual competitions are by far the safest "schooling" possible for horse and rider and provide a self-imposed discipline. The atmosphere of distraction at events—dogs, crowds, umbrellas, noise, fence judges on the course, and more, is an important factor in any conditioning program. For getting a horse fit, mentally and physically, nothing will ever replace competition.

During the final three weeks before the three-day competition, I recommend an almost daily two-hour walk to prepare the horse for the length of time he will have to carry the rider on his back on endurance day. Besides increasing the strength of weight-carrying muscles, this also aids in maintaining a very fit horse's mental balance. Also, at a competition, these long walks can replace turnout.

I cannot emphasize enough the need to listen to your horse. Take time to examine him thoroughly. Review your recent training schedule for indications of mental or physical excess. Remember, the horse has not chosen to do this sport, you have chosen for him. Mental and physical stress indicators are there if you take the time to read them.

Conditioning is a *must* for competition. You have to do it, and you must make the horse work. Fitness and soundness are crucial if you want to participate in eventing safely. Keep looking at your horse.

If a horse gets into trouble at a competition, if there is any trouble with his tendons, it may not show until five days afterward. The fitter the horse is, the longer it will take for a problem to show, particularly in the tendons. The problem will show only when he starts to relax after the competition. An unfit horse will demonstrate a leg problem very quickly (other than an accident).

Tendon problems are caused by two different factors. The first one is accidental. For instance, a horse landing wrong from a jump overextends and stretches the tendon, creating fiber breaks. Or, the horse can hit his front tendon with the hind leg while galloping. The second factor is due to lack of conditioning. The heart muscle is not capable of supplying enough clean blood to properly irrigate the tendon, which has little irrigation to begin with. As a result, the tendons are swollen and hot and the horse will break down.

TAKE RESPONSIBILITY

Check the legs and particularly the tendons every day as a routine before work. Touch the tendons with your fingers, but use the palm of your hand to feel heat. Don't just look, feel! Feel the legs every day. Don't leave it all to the groom when tacking him up. You are responsible. Don't transfer the responsibility. You must know your horse, how his legs look and feel when they are healthy. How will you know that something is wrong if you don't know what he looks like when he is right?

Stable management is also an imperative factor to success in the horse world and the example young riders see when in training with a true professional horseman will stick with them later when they are out on their own. Every horseman has a few tricks up his sleeve, and one should share them with his pupils. Before my father died, he took the time to teach me one or two things. One that comes to mind is how to treat splints. Splints are common on horses' legs, and they can have a drastic impact on his career.

I will share this with you now. As soon as you discover that your horse has a splint then:

1. Stop his training.

2. Shave close to the skin of the affected area.

3. Go to the butcher or supermarket and buy a good piece of fat back or lard (uncooked of course) from a pig.

4. Take all the fat away leaving just the thin filament of white membrane.

5. Cut a piece of this membrane large enough to cover the area of the splint and apply fat side to the splint.

6. Cover this with aluminum foil and wrap with sheet cotton and a stable wrap.

This should stay in place for two days. Rewrap the leg each day to make sure that everything stays in place. Keep in place for two days and then take it all off for one or two days. Then reapply fresh pig skin and rewrap. Repeat this process two or three times. Hand-walk the horse only. Some horses will literally blister. After 10 days of this treatment the horse can be returned to light work, but make sure that you protect his legs with good boots or bandages so that he does not hit the splint. The splint will go away in about three weeks if properly managed and if the splint is not old and cold. My success rate has been 95 percent.

Of course, I shared this with my younger brother when he began his riding career. Pierre was seven years younger than me and was brilliant. He was a graduate of St. Cyr (the French West Point) and was a career officer and an extremely promising one at that. After returning from the Algerian war, he entered the Cadre Noir in Saumur. I was then coach of the French Team based in Fontainebleau. Very late one night, I received a call from Pierre. He was all excited and told me, "I am reading some old books from the cavalry school, and guess what? Here it is printed about the pigskin treatment for splints." The books were two or three centuries old! A lot of those old horsemen's secrets were transmitted by word of mouth from generation to generation.

If your horse works right, if he is happy, and if you have prepared him for his job then you know what? He will win for you. Always use your head and your sensitivity when you work with horses! Remember horses and humans are on different wavelengths: they will never be on your wavelength but you have it in your power to get on theirs.

20

ON PREPARING FOR CROSS-COUNTRY

Before I begin, I want you to keep one thing in mind: Every horse is born with just so many miles and so many jumps in him. *Do not waste them!*

EARLY SCHOOLING

Horses should not know that a refusal is an option. So, when they come to an obstacle, they should figure out how to jump it, rather than thinking that stopping is an option available to them. That means you have to make sure that when you are schooling, you have to be certain that he is going to jump the fence, and you are not taking the chance that he can learn that stopping or running out is an option. That means you must not over face your horse. I am proud to say that I have ridden and trained several horses that retired having never refused to jump at home as well as in competition.

Also, it's important for the rider's confidence to know that while on the course he can trust the horse to try his best to jump the fence. Otherwise, the rider will be sitting between two chairs!

Start teaching your horse to jump by working over cavalletti, first at the walk and then by trotting over them—slowly. Then school him over a variety of small fences at the trot. Schooling over low fences will build the horse's confidence. Then repeat this exercise at the canter. Remember, never force your horse over high fences as he will lose his confidence. Move out of the ring into the schooling field and add some ditches, banks, drops, water jumps, and bullfinches to the ordinary fences and when you are both comfortable and jumping these with ease, you are both ready for some more serious cross-country schooling.

For an event horse, as soon as you are ready to jump single fences from a canter, you should go out on the cross-country course and pop over all kinds of different fences, little ditches, banks up and down, going through the water, and so on. If you have a friend with an experienced horse go with him and follow him over the natural fences, this is the next best thing to foxhunting.

REQUIREMENTS FOR CROSS-COUNTRY RIDING

Five conditions must be met to jump cross-country fences efficiently:

1. Direction (the track to be followed and the trajectory over the jumps including angles).

2. Speed (cadence and rhythm).

3. Balance.

4. Impulsion.

5. Timing.

These five conditions are a fairly good order of priority for an event horse. For a show jumper, the timing moves right to the top with direction and speed since the jumpers are asked to jump from a flat surface over fences pretty much at their maximum jumping ability. Rarely is an event horse going cross-country asked to jump to his maximum scope and ability. So if his approach and line to the fence are right, the speed is appropriate, and his balance and impulsion are adequate, the chances are that even if the timing is not perfect, it is very likely going to work out. You will see horses putting one more or one less stride in combinations and being perfectly safe, particularly when cross-country fences are on uneven terrain.

The Importance of Direction

My friend, Olympic show jumper and coach to the United States Show Jumping Team George Morris, insists that the riders use their eyes properly. He calls it "eye control" and I could not agree more. Whether it is on the flat in a dressage ring, in a show-jumping ring, or on a cross-country course, the eyes are the first and most important tool that a rider has. Most of my life, I have heard instructors yelling, "Keep your eyes up." Of course, that is true, but do their students know why they are being asked to do this? There is more to it than just saying the words. The eyes should anticipate the track you are following for jumping fences, just enough to make sure you are on the track you walked for riding your course. In dressage, your eyes should be *only* a few strides ahead as the speed is slow and you know the geometry of the figures in the dressage arena. If you turn your head too much to one side, you are likely to get your horse off the track that you are supposed to follow. One word of caution: your head weighs between 20 and 30 pounds. If you move your head over to one side or the other, you will totally alter the balance, the direction, and the straightness. So if you have a bad habit of tilting your head, then I say "get rid of it!" The habit, that is.

I have said for years that horses will follow your eyes. Nothing is truer because your eyes dictate the desired position needed to make a turn to the rest of your body. Consequently, it has a significant influence on your weight and balance. I have repeatedly used the example of a racecar going downhill as fast as possible and asked students to think what would happen if the driver took his eyes off the road ahead.

There is also one other imperative factor that is related to the use of the eyes and that is the sense of balance. Without getting too involved in physics, let's accept that the center of gravity is directly under our feet. When moving forward on a horse, the balance is obviously always moving forward directly under you at a 90-degree angle. So if you keep your eyes on that 90-degree angle relative to the ground (center of gravity), you are in the best place to detect if your horse is speeding up, slowing down, or changing his balance or direction. Please experiment. Look down first and see where the center of gravity is, then raise your eyes directly in front of you and look straight ahead so your line of sight is parallel to the ground. This line will always put you at a 90-degree angle from your center of gravity and down to the ground. I would be surprised if you could not feel a remarkable difference. It is like riding a bicycle or driving a car: you will be able to feel, as well as see, whether the horse is staying on a straight line and whether he increases his speed or slows down. I guarantee you will feel it.

Observing horses teaches you a lot of things. When a horse is jumping please concentrate on his eyes and you will be able to tell at which precise moment he sees the jump. You will then see him react to that jump: he will run to it, slow down, or avoid it. The sooner the horse sees the fence, the sooner he will react to it and the more time the rider has to adjust his riding to the horse's reaction and make the necessary corrections for a successful jump. So get his eyes on the fence as soon as you can.

This is especially true with a young horse, and he needs to be trained to look at a fence early. People have often heard me shout, "Get his eyes on the jump!" The best way to do this is to get him straight in his neck between the reins. A young horse gets easily distracted and only three or four strides from the jump he will be looking at something, anything, other than the jump.

At the opposite end of the spectrum, you can observe a show jumper in a jump-off or speed class, and you will see that the horse is trying to identify the fence you are coming to jump. The cycle of "your brain to your body, your body to his brain, and his brain to his body" is still taking place but much more quickly than with a young horse. (Remember, this cycle takes a little time to complete and you should make your preparations early enough so that the horse has time to process the request.) We all have seen young horses with lots of scope and talent ruined because they were asked to jump big fences early on. They had the physical ability to do it, but mentally were not ready to process the cycle fast enough and identify the size and difficulty of the jump in front of them.

Of course, every horse is a little bit different and can be easily separated into categories: the "rushers," the "timids" that do not want to attack their fences and slow down to put in an extra stride before take-off, and the "stoppers." This latter group is somewhat related to the timids, and a proper schooling session might remedy some of these problems, but let's face it, some horses are just not born to be jumping fences.

One remedy I have tried for the horse that rushes to his jumps is to take back on landing, turn and walk as soon as possible. If on the contrary, he is timid, I will send him forward a few strides upon landing. After repeating these precise corrections, the horse will start to anticipate what is going to happen after landing and will begin to react before the fence to what is coming. This will make him more rideable. Again, the aim should always be to "get his eyes on the fence" as soon as possible.

THE IMPORTANCE OF CORRECT SPEED

Speed is very important. When you play a game, you have to know the rules. If you don't know what your speed can be and is, you will just go over the speed required, or go too slowly. Horses that travel at appropriate speeds are less apt to get hurt and are more apt to go clean. Unnecessary speed makes horses excited and disobedient. It doesn't make any sense to go faster than is safe. The right speed is very important for each level of competition. You do not get more points by going faster than the speed requirement.

You must not go into a fence taking back. When riders are coming into the fence taking back, it is riding backward: it makes the horse pull more toward the jump. In cross-country in particular, the horse has to have a chance to see the jump and the terrain leading up to it. You must not mess around with your hands at this point.

The speed changes with the particular fence. A spread takes more momentum. The horse needs impulsion over the fence. Regulate the speed between the fences and go with the horse at the fence, when necessary. But remember, go in slower if there is a slide or drop or water on the far side of the jump. You cannot go into these types of jumps at speed. Remember, a horse can easily jump 2½ or 3 feet from a trot provided he has impulsion. The ideal situation in which you want to find yourself coming into cross-country jumps is to have your horse between the jump and your legs rather than your hands and your legs, that is, the horse looking at those jumps will balance himself, and you just have to ride him to it. Most times, the timing works just by itself.

BALANCE

What is balance? We first have to understand that the balance will be different depending on whether we are in a dressage ring with the horse being asked to piaffe. His balance will be very much on the haunches. At the opposite end of the spectrum, is the racehorse running on the flat. His balance is a lot more on the forehand. The position of the rider varies according to what he is asking the horse to do. For instance, in the piaffe, the rider will sit deeper in the saddle, his back will be straighter, and his stirrups will be longer. When racing on the flat, the rider will have the most forward position with very short stirrups. In between these two extremes, there is show jumping, cross-country, and steeplechasing. The position of the rider and the lengths of the stirrups will be adjusted. The balance of the horse will also vary accordingly. We should also know that some horses are more naturally balanced than others. But this is also where training comes in as we talk about teaching horses to balance themselves going downhill.

CREATING IMPULSION

Impulsion is the horse's desire to move forward. If your horse has impulsion, you only need to allow your hands to go forward, and he will move forward. Remember to keep your legs close to his sides at all times. The rider regulates direction and the speed with his hands, but he must create the impulsion with his legs. Be able to feel your horse with your calves, just feel, not squeeze. You must teach your horse to accept the feel of your leg all the time, just as he was taught to accept the feel of the saddle. You have to use your leg in a progressive manner to get the desired reaction from the horse. We start with the horse accepting the contact of your leg on his side. The progression is "Press" (not squeeze), "Tap," "Kick," and "Bang." When the old expression says, "Kick on," that's what it means. But here again the training and what I call "the tuning up of the horse to the leg" is primordial and rather easy to do. Take your horse into a large arena. Ask him to go forward *at the canter only*. By tapping on his side with your legs, increase your legs' action to banging, if necessary, with possibly the help of a whip. Repeat this exercise several times paying attention to turning your reins loose so it is clear to him that it is legs without reins. At some point, the fourth or sixth time of repeating the exercise, you should feel your horse ready to go forward with very little help from your legs. This is called the "Lesson of the Leg."

CHOOSING THE CORRECT LINE

Sometimes you may have to jump a corner for time purposes. Pick your line early and stick with it; you hope you can see your distance early enough to come forward to that corner. You must be very precise in going toward it. You should be in full control of the direction even in the air. Be a pilot, not a passenger. When I was riding in the Rome Olympics in 1960 there was a very difficult fence at the end of the course (see Photo 12). It consisted of a huge ditch. The revetting of the ditch, if you could call it that, had given way as horse after horse missed the landing side and scrambled to stay upright. When I walked the course, I had the line fixed in my mind, but as I came up to the fence on my horse Image, I saw that the red flag had been moved over to the middle of the fence. In a split second, I had to size up a new line, put my horse on to this line and hold it until we were over. I saw out of the corner of my eye a dead horse in the ditch, the real reason they had to move the flags. If I hadn't known the course well enough and hadn't had complete confidence in my ability to ride a line and the obedience of my horse to stay on the line, I am not sure we would have got over that fence. Many didn't.

JUMPING DITCHES, WATER JUMPS, AND BANKS

At a ditch, water jump, or bank, interfere as little as possible with your horse. Regulate the speed and the direction, but leave him with some initiative. On these jumps the horse must do this himself, especially going up banks. Increase speed, but don't increase the stride. A shorter stride gets you to the right take-off point more easily. Look at the point of take-off you desire. For once, look down at this point as you approach the fence. It will help you keep your weight forward, and your horse will be less apt to jump standing back. And we always end up going where we are looking!

When jumping into water, do not come in too fast because your horse could trip in the water and lose his balance. Most times the fall happens after the landing stride.

Going up banks, stay close to the saddle with your legs and seat, and stay forward. Don't try to dictate the stride. Going down banks, keep your legs on the girth and close them tight to straighten your back a little and keep your balance when landing. If you sit too far back going down a bank, you may get a kick in the pants with the saddle cantle. Stay forward as much as you can so as not to lose your balance and still be safe.

WALK THE COURSE THREE TIMES

Walk the cross-country course three times, if possible. Walk it the first time with the crowd at the official opening of the course. It will be difficult to concentrate at this time, but you should get a general idea of the course, of the direction and lay of the land. Don't waste this first walk, but just try to get a feel for the whole course.

The second time, walk it with your coach. Study the fences one by one. Study your approach and pick the best one. Pick your line by deciding which line will work best. Study how the fence is presented; it will influence your choice of approach and how to jump it. Study the options and be prepared to take them if Plan A does not work.

The third time, go alone. Walk out the lines you will ride as decided in your second walk. Have it well in mind before you start. You will profit by riding the course just as you have walked it. On this walk, pick out landmark trees you can head for from a distance. Know where your fences are from these landmarks and what the distances are so you will know whether to go around a blind turn strong or in good control for a rapidly approaching fence.

Memorize your course as you will ride it, and know it by heart.

DOUBLE CHECK YOUR EQUIPMENT

Go over your equipment thoroughly before your ride to see that all of it is in good shape. As you head out toward the starting area, go over it all again, seeing that all the adjustments are properly made to your girth, bit, boots, spurs, martingale, and stirrup length. Be sure you know the rules, especially regarding combinations. The main rule is to go clear over every jump the first time. Enjoy yourself.

21

ON SHOW JUMPING

There are two vital parts to riding. One is educating the rider—teaching him or her how to ride. The second is educating the horse, and you should never have a beginner riding a green horse. My axiom has always been, "An older horse with a younger rider (and here I make no reference to the age of the rider) and an older rider with a younger horse." I must emphasize, this applies to all types of riding, not just show jumping.

For the serious rider who wishes to learn well it is best to use a school horse whose competition days are over. The competing horse must never be sacrificed for the sake of teaching the rider how to ride. The competing horse must take priority, and his education comes before all else. Unfortunately, today there are fewer and fewer facilities with school horses. Riders have to learn on their competition horses, which can sometimes be to the detriment of the horse's education. Plus, the amount of riding a beginner will need to do requires many hours in the saddle, and you couldn't ask just one horse to do that much work. So riders would be best to look for instructors who can provide good school horses, to allow for the necessary riding time as well as to get the best riding education.

The process of training the horse to jump can start as soon as you have reasonable control of the speed and direction. In other words, when your horse responds fairly well to being asked to go forward, come back, and turn.

CAVALLETTI TRAINING

The simplest form of jumps are cavalletti. Once the horse can walk over one and then trot over it, I like to set up five cavalletti in a straight line 4 feet 6 inches apart. At first, I pull numbers 2 and 4 out of the line and make the horse walk and then trot over those two. Then I make the horse walk, then trot over cavalletti 1, 3, and 5. After that, I bring in 2 and 4 and make the horse trot, not walk, over all 5. Do not let the horse jump them; he must trot them.

Very soon I ask the horse to trot over at a working trot. For the more experienced horses, when they are comfortable with this exercise on a straight line I set up the cavalletti on a curving line. I use the corner of the arena and set them using a 20-meter circle as the basis for placement. The cavalletti are set on the line of the radius from the center point of the circle. It is of the utmost importance that the distances between the rails are very precise. The distance from one cavalletto to another on a line through the center should be 4 feet 6 inches. On an outside line, the distance will be no more than 6 feet and on the inside line no more than 3 feet 3 inches. These precise distances will give you the opportunity to work the horse through at a normal stride in the center and then lengthen the stride on the outside and shorten on the inside according to what your horse needs. Please note that the cavalletti on a curve require a well-schooled horse-and-rider combination and should not be used with a green horse. It is a great test of good riding.

There are numerous benefits to training over cavalletti and in my book the most important one is the mental impact on the horse's mind. As I have said, cavalletti are the simplest form of jump, and tackling several cavalletti in a row is the simplest form of a combination. It is essential to make sure of your distances, as the horse will quickly realize that he can comfortably go over all those rails on that line without losing his mind, or as I like to say, "bicycling through the sauerkraut."

Another benefit of using cavalletti is the balance developed through the coordination of the rider's aids regulating the horse's rhythm. This brings cadence to the trot and is a good exercise for the top line. For me, though, it is the mental and psychological benefits that are at the top of my list and the development of obedience to the rider's aids.

While I was at Gladstone from 1970 to 1974, I saw possibly the best master in the world using cavalletti and gymnastic work for the show jumpers. His systematic method of training the young horses as well as refreshing the international-caliber horses made me realize that it is not only a way to educate your young horses, but it also provides an excellent return to the fundamentals for the Grand Prix horses that have been chased at speed in jump-offs against the clock all season. Of course, I had used cavalletti and gymnastics in Europe before coming to the States, but if I needed to be convinced of the value of the principle, I certainly got that by watching Bert de Némethy. He was not only a master of that but also of longeing horses over jumps. What a privilege!

I know that a lot of people use gymnastics following a cavalletti line. I did try this for a while, thinking that if it was used by so many people, then it had to be okay. After a very thorough try, too many times I saw a horse missing a step in the cavalletti line and being in real trouble when he tried to tackle the gymnastic. Being the firm believer that I am in both exercises, I separated the two.

For the gymnastic line, I use a placing ground rail before the first jump and have my line of gymnastic fences that are essentially oxers. Oxers work for the more experienced horses though I often use a cross-rail as a first fence, and then a vertical for the younger ones as that leads the horse to the center of the first jump and helps him stay centered all the way through. The distance between the jumps (and for oxers this is essential) is critical. For a one stride, the jumps will be 18 feet apart, 28 to 30 feet apart for two strides, and 39 to 41 feet for three strides, according to your horse. All distances are measured from inside the rails. The placing pole will be 9 feet from the first jump.

There are a variety of exercises with gymnastics that can be performed. *The De Némethy Method: Modern Techniques for Training the Show Jumper and Its Rider* by former USET Coach Bertalan de Némethy (Xenophon Press, 2016), which describes these exercises and their benefits, is the best book you can acquire on this topic.

Once the horse is confident over gymnastic lines and assuming that he is a young horse, I start trotting him over a lot of different types of small fences. Next, I canter these same fences but one at a time. First, canter a single fence, and make sure the horse is confident. When he has confidently cantered the single fence keep the canter and move on to another fence but not at a related distance. The jumping sessions should be short, but you can do them two to three times a week. Gradually, over several jumping sessions, you should be able to jump several non-related fences and then finally put together an easy type of low hunter course.

At the point where your horse is ready to jump individual fences at the canter, get into the habit of picking up the canter from the walk (after a proper warm-up) and after the jumps, come back to a walk from the canter—avoid the trot. There is no competition for jumping at the trot, and the jump is just a canter stride over a fence so get used to it as soon as possible!

APPLYING IT
When "dressage," "schooling," and "training," (all the same thing for me) are done correctly and are a fundamental part of the horse's

education, there should not be one way to ride in the dressage ring, a second way in the show-jumping ring, and yet a third way on the cross-country course. I am very clear in my mind that we should be able to use the straight dressage training for jumping fences. Going back to the dressage for a precise exercise at the canter:

1. Lengthen the stride and shorten the stride (young horses).

2. Extended canter to collected canter (experienced horses).

If you know that an average stride for an average horse at say the working canter is 12 feet, then through proper training, you should be able to get your horse doing an 8-foot stride at the collected canter, and a 15- to 16-foot stride at the extended canter. This is what I believe riding is all about: going forward, coming back, and turning. You cannot adjust the distance to your stride, but the flat work you have done on your horse should allow you to adjust your stride to that distance.

PRACTICE WILL MAKE YOU PERFECT

We all know that the two essential basics of eventing are dressage and show jumping. More so than ever before and probably more so in the years to come, dressage and show jumping are the dividing factors between the winner and the rest of the field.

The eventing dressage tests are getting more demanding, and the quality of the horses and the riding is getting better and better. Event show jumping is moving more and more towards real show jumping, thank God! I remember the old days of Badminton when the show-jumping courses were so poor the final phase totally bored the public. Today, the size of the fences has increased, and I am very proud that I had something to do with it because when I wrote the rules and regulations for the Eventing World Cup, I increased the height to 1.25 meters with a 5-centimeter tolerance. This allowed the course designers to have a meaningful show-jumping course.

Not surprisingly, the horses jumped better, and the riders have made real progress in their riding. Of course, the public now loves it because the suspense is there until the last horse and the last jump, just as in real show jumping.

There is no doubt that riders aspiring to be top class will have to get deeper into the dressage work and definitely have to practice and compete much more in show jumping than they are doing today. Mark Todd, Vaughn Jefferis, and Blyth Tait all competed in pure show jumping while also competing in eventing. "Toddy" even rode on the New Zealand Show Jumping Team at the Olympic Games at the same time he was on the Eventing Team! Their prowess in this discipline has many times helped them clinch victories in eventing that they would otherwise have missed. By comparison, the typical US eventer goes to few dressage shows and even fewer show-jumping competitions.

Now let's take an example. A lucky event rider may have two horses competing and possibly one or two young ones coming up. With his two competing horses, he might go to six or seven events during the season. If everything is okay and the horses stay sound, that means the rider has ridden a maximum of 15 show-jumping courses during that season. How does he expect to be relaxed and efficient in the jumping with only 15 show-jumping rounds to his record?

A show jumper gets more rounds in one horse show than the event rider does in one whole year. The conclusion is very evident: event riders have to go to more dressage shows and jumper shows. Furthermore, they must train with a good dressage trainer and a good show-jumping trainer. They should not be concerned about being disloyal to their eventing trainer. Any professional, and I mean *professional*, trainer in any discipline will encourage his students to gain as much knowledge and experience as they possibly can. Just as it is with children, if you let them explore and test their wings they will always return to you, especially when it comes time to walk that cross-country course!

22

ON THE RIDERS

I believe there are three categories of riders. A good dozen of them are the cream of the cream. Some stay on top of their game for a few years and a handful of them dominate the sport for a decade or more. Those who come to mind are Mark Todd, Pippa Funnell, William Fox-Pitt, Andrew Nicholson, David and Karen O'Connor, Kim Severson, Bruce Davidson Sr., Andrew and Bettina Hoy, Jean Teuleure and a smattering of others.

A few years ago, Richard Meade, Tad Coffin, Lucinda Green, Ginny Leng (now Elliott), and Mike Plumb dominated their era, along with a dozen or so other top-class riders.

The top-class riders of today would have been top class in those former years just as those riders back then would have been top class today. Quite simply it is because they are the best and regardless of what format of competition you put before them they will be the best no matter what.

In the second category, there are around 40 or 50 serious riders. They are the good, consistent professionals. From time to time, they win competitions. They are known to the public and place well in general.

The third category is the biggest one. These riders often compete with only a few successful results, but they enjoy the atmosphere of the event. They make up the bulk of the starting list when the competitions are not restricted.

A Rider of Rare Talent

In addition to the three categories I've mentioned, there is one on its own, and that category is reserved for Mark Todd. I have said many times that he has been parachuted from another planet. He is the most talented rider I have ever met in my life. Sure, I have judged him many times, but I also have observed and watched him when not judging, and this fellow can do it all: dressage, steeple-chase (exceedingly well given his 6 feet 4 inches height) and show jumping. I honestly believe that he would have been as successful if he concentrated on dressage. Of course, he has managed to compete successfully in show jumping and was on the Olympic Show Jumping Team for New Zealand as well as their Three-Day Event Olympic team.

His communication with horses is exceptional. He gives them confidence. I will never forget Toddy riding at Badminton on a horse he had sat on for the first time that week. I don't think he had hardly jumped a fence on the horse. He went out early in the day on one of the tougher Badminton courses and made it look easy. The riders and coaches were watching on the closed-circuit television in the 10-minute box and thought, "Well we got it wrong, the course is much easier than we thought." Well, the day went on, and riders were crashing and burning everywhere! Only Mark Todd could have put on such a performance.

On the other hand, I have had to deal with many very different types of riders over the course of my professional career:

- The Lovers: Jean-Jacques Guyon (gold medal individual in Mexico), Tad Coffin, Don Sachey, and a couple of others. These were the romantics; they had an easygoing and gentle temperament.

- The Fighters: Bruce Davidson, Mike Plumb, Torrance Watkins, and Kevin Freeman.

- The Thinkers: Jim Wofford, David O'Connor, and a couple of others.

Few are Fighters *and* Thinkers, but if they are, they become the best. Kim Severson is a classic example of this type of rider.

Overall, I had a great time working with all of the riders in all their shapes, sizes, and personalities. Each one is different, and you have to approach them differently. The goal, at least mine, was to make them ride well: to ride their horses properly and thoroughly, with no gimmicks. The big advantage for me was that any rider can ride any horse if they have all been trained the same way. By having the riders ride the same way and having the horses trained the same way I could change the combinations around without too much of a problem.

THE HORSE COMPONENT

As I have said earlier, up until the Mexico Olympics in 1968, the US three-day riders were mainly riding team horses. One or two riders owned theirs, and some had sponsors who bought them horses to ride. The team had some horses, not many, and they were extremely useful in teaching the riders how to ride and compete. Few were good enough to make the team, but Plain Sailing, Chalan, Foster, Bally Cor, Good Mixture, Blue Stone, and Golden Griffin were able to go to the Olympics, the World Championships, and the Pan American Games and win. Because there were seldom more than five or six horses owned by the team, they provided an excellent return on our money. Then times changed, and it was harder to find supporters to donate money to buy horses. More often, riders came to the team with their own horses, and not all of those horses were of international potential, believe me. I will share with you an example of what I mean.

As I have mentioned, when I stopped coaching after the Los Angeles Games, I continued as Director of the USET Training Center in Hamilton, Massachusetts. I was developing up-and-coming riders whom I spotted either at a competition or clinic. One such rider had an acceptable horse, not an easy horse, but he was okay. More than anything I believed in the young jockey. His name? David O'Connor.

In 1986, many people could not afford to go to the World Championships held in Gawler, Australia so an additional CCIO competition was organized at Bialy Bor in Poland. The US sent a team to Gawler, but it was impossible for the team to fund a trip for David to go abroad to Bialy Bor; the money simply was not available, and his horse's performance did not justify going to bat for it. I believed that it was a good thing to do. Well, I was not wealthy by any means, but I dug down into my pocket, and that made it easier for me to go and ask all the neighborhood friends to pitch in to send David and Border Raider to Poland. To make a long story short, David did a super job for the US and was second to Britain's Ginny Leng. That was very rewarding for all involved and the beginning of David's international career. And how well he went on to prove that they were right to believe in him!

In the United States, there is no school of riding where people can immerse themselves for months and even years in the art of classical equitation as I had done with the Cadre Noir. Yes, there are riding schools and colleges that offer equine degrees, but the riders do not devote themselves purely to learning the art of riding, nor are they given as much help as they need to compete internationally or to coach international teams. To my knowledge, the Morven Park International Equestrian School was the last one that had a goal like this. In Europe, these schools still exist in several countries, and when the riders have a solid base in the correct techniques of riding then the aspect of competing becomes a great deal easier later on.

It takes several years to learn how to ride, and there are no shortcuts in good riding. The most successful riders take lessons for most of their lives. I remember Bill Steinkraus, long after winning his Olympic gold medal in show jumping in Mexico, coming to Gladstone and working on the longe line before a jumping session. So, young riders, there is nothing babyish or inferior about being on a longe line. In fact, the more hours you spend on it, the better you will be.

Training people for an extended period should not be limited to teaching them how to ride. When a rider is in your custody almost 24/7, you have a responsibility to teach him or her also about life, to be honest, to be a good sportsman, to have respect for others. These riders are fairly young, and everything you teach them will help them in their future professional life. It is not an easy task, but often you are a little bit like a second parent. Of course, I am happy and very proud to think I have contributed somewhat to the achievements of riders like David O'Connor and several others. It makes you feel good and when there is time to reflect you only wish you could have done more.

MAKING HORSES

Kilkenny was Tommy Brennan's horse from Ireland. Tommy was on the Irish Olympic Team in Mexico, and Jimmy Wofford had seen the horse there, fallen for him, and he bought him.

Some of the riders buy "made" horses as they have a theory that it costs less to buy one sure thing than to buy several young ones only to find out only one is going to make it. If you, or someone you know, have the financial wherewithal to do this and you can persuade them to buy the horse, then it is a valid way to go. However, there is nothing like the satisfaction of starting a horse off at the beginning of his career and ending with him at the four-star level.

I believe that in eventing there are two types of workers: the pilot, and the mechanic. The pilot "flies" or rides the horse, and the mechanic prepares him and makes sure he is fit, trained, and ready to compete. The horseman does both; he trains the horse and competes him.

Bruce Davidson is exceptional in this regard. He has made almost all of his horses and taken them to the top. David O'Connor is a true horseman and having spent four-and-half years with me I am proud to see him train his horses on a daily basis when they are young. He and his wife Karen work together to bring the young ones on, and there will be a great many exceptionally well-trained horses in the sport thanks to them.

I talk a bit more about a few of the champion riders I had the pleasure of working with in a special section at the end of this book (see p. 225).

23

ON CROSS-COUNTRY COURSES

The evolution of Olympic cross-country courses from 1956 in Stockholm until today has been dramatic. To briefly summarize, Stockholm was an old-fashioned course, unpolished in many ways, and the building of the obstacles was quite rudimentary. Rome was a big, long course with the introduction of a bounce into the water over thin rails, overall a very tough course. Tokyo had a good variety of fences, but it was not big. Mexico will always remain marred because of the torrential rain, which essentially changed the course from one hour to the next. It also had a huge steeplechase. Munich was probably the beginning of the new era, with lots of alternatives, maybe too many. There we began to see fences that were polished and well presented. Montreal was not a big course but the terrain, including the roads and tracks, made it more difficult than it was. The concept was more of a Pony Club course brought up to international size. Fontainebleau, the alternative Olympics to Moscow, was big and challenging enough and a bit twisty. Los Angeles was very much in line with the progression toward sophisticated obstacles with great carpentry work, and a concerted effort made to create an attractive presentation throughout the entire course. Barcelona in 1992 was based on the same idea as the 1982 World Championships in Luhmuhlen, Germany—lots of alternatives and the carpentry was almost like cabinetwork. There were almost three courses for the riders to pick from, all beautifully presented, and there we saw the start of the trend for jumping keyholes cut out of brush. It was big but fair.

Atlanta ended up being a very good cross-country course. A competition was organized on the same grounds the year preceding the Olympics. The purpose was to test the cross-country conditions, terrain, etc. It proved to be a very valuable exercise as we learned a lot from that event regarding managing the competition horse in high heat and humidity. This information coupled with the research done by the USCTA and the findings and suggestions from the FEI Veterinary Committee appointed for that purpose gave us a chance to be well prepared to cope with possible drastic weather conditions. There were several Plan Bs elaborated, which could be put into effect if the heat was a dangerous factor for the horses.

During the Olympic Games the Ground Jury of four judges, Lord Patrick Carew, Bernd Springorum, General Nane Grignolo and I, in total cooperation with the Technical Delegate Hugh Thomas, the course designer Roger Haller, and the Veterinarian Commission reviewed the situation every day of the competition. This knowledgeable group of officials was ready to go to one of the Plan Bs if necessary. From the competition point of view, it was a great success. The two cross-country courses, individual, and team, worked very well. The cooling procedures with fans and mist were terrific. I have to mention that it is the only time in my long career as an FEI judge that I had several chefs d'equipe from different countries coming to me wanting to congratulate my fellow judges and me on the standard of dressage judging and all the other decisions made. *Wow!* I wish I could say the same about the organization of the Games (see p. 134).

Sydney was an excellent Olympics altogether. Now we clearly saw the introduction of narrow fences, even on an angle. Corner fences appeared in the late 80s and were the first accuracy questions. Badminton had some over ditches that made you wonder how the horses were going to tackle them.

Over the years, the courses went from unpolished, basic, and not very attractive to having huge wide fences that you had to jump at speed. The scope of the horse and the heart of the rider were the necessary ingredients to be successful over these types of courses. Then more combinations appeared, mainly in a straight line, and the course designer had to find ways to separate the very good riders from the good riders. From straight-line combinations, we progressed to combinations on turns requiring more accurate riding, and now we are trending to extremely narrow fences where accuracy is in high demand.

How would the riders of 30 years ago do over these courses? At first, they would be shocked, but the good ones would adapt very quickly.

How about the horses? Well, I think the majority of horses we were riding back then would be in trouble, simply because they would not be good enough to cope. The quality of the horses we see today is 100 percent better those 30 to 40 years ago. A good portion of them would be good as show jumpers, dressage horses, and steeplechasers. Of course, there were some good ones then but few and far between. A lot of them were army horses, not good enough to show jump or do pure dressage. In the sport of eventing, I think that it is the type of horse that has had the most dramatic change in the last 40 to 50 years.

Eventing has become very sophisticated, and there is no room for mediocrity. Of course, I am speaking of the international level. The top riders have several horses at the three- and four-star levels. They compete a lot more often riding more than one horse. In the 1950s and 60s if you had three to four international events to go to that was about all you could do in a given year. Today's riders compete in 15 to 20 competitions per year, often riding several horses in each one. Their experience riding cross-country is making them sharper and obviously, as a consequence, they have learned how to condition their horses more precisely for each competition.

PART V

The Past and the Future

"If you keep expending energy fighting
to go back, you will miss the boat."

24

THE CROSSING OF THE DESERT: THE US THREE-DAY EVENT TEAM 1984–1996

At this point, I would like to address what happened to the US Three-Day Event Team after I left in 1984 and until 1996.

Experience has shown that to produce successful teams, eventing, as well as every other sport, needs consistent and regular support from coaches and trainers. Immediately after my retirement as coach the US Three-Day Team won the Team gold and individual silver medals at the 1984 Olympic Games in Los Angeles, there was a period when the riders felt that they could do without a coach. The team went from number one in the world to number 10, or something like that.

The team entered what I like to call a "10-year crossing of the desert" when no one was in charge, a period of drought regarding international success, where they seemed to be just staggering through the motions of being competitive. It was a barren period for US eventing and in my opinion, it was directly related to the lack of a real coach.

Now I believe in democracy but guided democracy. After all, someone has to be in charge, and the buck has to stop somewhere. It is inconceivable to have a football, basketball, or a hockey team without a coach but that is what happened to the US team. And the results spoke for themselves. The best we could do in Seoul was to finish two riders. The team was eliminated. Phyllis Dawson put up a great effort to be the highest placed American by finishing tenth on Albany II. Bruce Davidson and Dr. Peaches were behind her in eighteenth. Our other two riders were eliminated or retired on cross-country.

Also, the riders were significantly affected by the overall development and success of the sport. Eventing was no longer a pure amateur hobby supported through the generosity of wealthy patrons and engaged in by those with both the time and financial support necessary to maintain a string of horses in top-level competition. Now it became a professional sport that was able to support businesses for those talented riders who could now make a real living out of their passion. This was good as it opened the door to many superb riders who previously had not had the means to engage in top-level competition due to financial and time constraints. It is very hard to work full time to support your horses and then find the long hours necessary to ride and train them, and many great riders have been left by the wayside through lack of funds.

SELF-DESTRUCTION?

I was fortunate in that I had been able to have the riders come to the team headquarters and spend many weeks and months riding and training. When we competed abroad, we were often gone for several weeks at a time, and the riders had to be free to do this. Toward the end, this was becoming increasingly difficult as many of them now had flourishing "eventing" businesses to run at home. They had clients to take care of, and many were in demand teaching clinics all over the country. They had working students and staffs to supervise horses in training and horses to be sold. No longer could they afford to be away from home week after week. In effect, the immense success of eventing in the United States had created a burgeoning industry which, if not handled carefully, had the power to destroy what had taken so many years to create—the United States as a dominant force on the eventing world scene.

Those in charge, therefore, felt that the riders could still be successful if allowed to work more independently, coming together for intensive training sessions under a coach for periods of time. Although one can understand the business and financial reasons both from the riders' and the team's perspectives, I felt that there was a great danger of losing that all-important team spirit.

Also significant was the potential loss of the coach's and trainer's personal knowledge of every horse. Good stable management and the care of the horse are essential. The team lost horses through unsoundness because the riders who came to the training sessions and received instructions from the chef d'equipe and the vet on how to treat their horse when they got home often did not follow up, and no one was monitoring them. Months later, the riders were still on their own, and the team lost horses.

As I said before, during my tenure, I knew each horse so intimately that if you blindfolded me and led out any horse, I could identify him simply by feeling his legs. Armed with such knowledge, I was able to work with the selectors and the veterinarians to determine which horses were at the peak of their conditioning and which were the healthiest, thereby standing the best chance of coming through all three phases of competition. This, of course, is the subjective side of producing winning teams. You must also have the objective side that looks for a consistently successful competition record during open compulsory selection trials.

It should be said that what was necessary and possible to produce a winning team in the 1970s is likely not feasible today. The whole situation of eventing in the United States is very different from those years. The evolution of the sport is in constant motion, and one has to adjust to it if you do not want to be left behind.

Also, for many athletes in many sports, a berth on an Olympic team means not only the honor of representing your country, which truly overrides all other reasons to this day but it now also brings financial rewards—when you win a gold medal your face might appear on the Wheaties box! The era of large dollar sponsorships was upon us. Some of the British and New Zealand riders were signing deals for tens of thousands of dollars, and that did not go unnoticed here in the United States.

This meant that the competition to make a team was fierce, and pressure was brought to bear upon the USET to make the selection process entirely objective. The USET responded in the spring of 1988 by stating that the first five horses in the Rolex Kentucky Three-Day Event (at the end of April) would make up the team for the Seoul Olympics in September.

LEGAL ACTION

Litigation, something I abhor, was also a fear that began to raise its head. Of course, everyone now knows that due to a broken leg sustained in a fall on her first horse, HMS Dash, our most successful horse-and-rider combination at that time, Kerry Millikin and The Pirate, were unable to compete in the selection trial that weekend and were therefore left off the team. Who knows if she would have been able to recover in time to produce The Pirate at his best for Seoul? Goodness knows I had faced a similar problem with Kim Walnes and the Gray Goose in 1982, but the selection process in place in 1988 would not allow for that kind of subjectivity. It is also impossible to determine if a horse at his supreme best both physically and mentally in April will be able to produce that same level of well-being five or six months later. A desperately disappointed Kerry brought legal action against the USET.

To add to its burdens, a show jumper who felt she had been wrongly left off the Show Jumping Team sued the USET, all of which forced the team to adopt a points-based selection process. That step proved to be less than successful given the poor results at the 1991 Pan American Championships and the 1992 Barcelona Olympic Games. Following the Games in Barcelona I wrote the following in the (then) *USCTA News* (December 1992):

"Selection by points simply doesn't work. It has been tried by other countries with no success. Many good horses are passed by, and the remaining good horses are used up by the time they get to the actual competition. Our US horses were competing in a three-day event just three months before the Olympics and were still competing for points for a team slot just two weeks before the Games in Barcelona. Preparation should be part of selection—they are almost one and the same. A good selection process should prepare the horses and riders. Selection by the process of elimination, although politically comfortable, is unreasonable. We have to adjust to the times, situations change and evolve. Above all, we must provide good judgment and a horseman's point of view in our selection process if we want to become a reckoning force in international eventing again.

"What it all comes down to is that we must have a selection process that makes sense and is fair. Before the selection process begins, the criteria must be made clear to the riders, and agreed upon in a legal document that all potential candidates would sign and abide by."

In that same article, I also stated that the US Team was lacking in leadership and recommended that a plan be put in place and the right people plugged in to implement the plan. I went on to say, "The leadership I am speaking of involves two people. One of these people would have a permanent job as a manager/director and would be responsible for all logistical preparations. The second person would be a coach responsible for the conception of the training program, and the progression and training of the horses and riders once they are selected for a particular competition. The coach and chef d'equipe should be the same person as the chef d'equipe at the competitions determines the "order of go." He should also know the horses and riders in depth, so as to maximize their training, knowledge, and skills. A coach's job is a difficult and lonely one—especially today as riders are under considerable stress and pressure, even more so now that sponsors are involved in requiring riders to justify money invested in them and their horses."

The following year, the US Team hired Jim Wolf as Director of Three-Day Eventing, and Captain Mark Phillips as coach and chef d'equipe. The results after that drastically improved and under Mark's guidance, the US once again rose to the very top of Olympic and international eventing. Individual bronze and team silver medals in the Atlanta Olympics; individual gold and team bronze in Sydney; team gold at the World Equestrian Games in Jerez in 2002; team gold and a clean sweep of the individual medals at the Pan Am Championships in 2003; and the individual silver and team bronze in Athens speak to the wisdom of having experienced and accomplished leaders and coaches at the helm.

25

WHERE THE SPORT IS GOING

At this writing, we have seen the Athens Olympics under the new formula. Although I was disappointed about the changes to the cross-country phase, we should still be happy to be in the Olympics. It was that formula—or we were out. Some people have not accepted this fact, and they will be left behind and miss the boat.

It is likely that the level of the course was the result of several factors and competitions preceding Athens. The 2004 Lexington CCI**** was an excellent course that year but the "CIC modified" was bad; there were about the same number of fences on both courses, but the CIC was over a much shorter distance. Of course, the horses in that division came back exhausted. Then the same mistake was made at Punchestown a few weeks later, and as a consequence, the Olympic course was much too easy. Then the Burghley CCI**** was massive and suffered from unfriendly weather conditions. In other words, the 2004 season was like a yo-yo—up and down.

The sport originated in the Army to test horses and riders for combat purposes. Some people wanted to keep the old three-day formula, hiding behind the big word "tradition." Out of curiosity, they should look at what was required in the first Olympics at the turn of the century, and I do not believe they would like to bring back that "tradition" for the endurance test. (Anyone who has ridden the 2,000-meter flat at the end of the cross-country does not miss that "tradition.")

Eventing today is a modern sport that has its roots in the military, but it is now a civilian sport practiced by young people, women, pure amateurs, and real professionals.

Some 25 years ago, I expressed my personal opinion about the endurance test. Again, I would like to say that I wish we could keep Badminton, Burghley, Lexington, and all top-class competitions like World, European, and Pan American Championships under the old formula. That being clearly expressed, I have never seen any merit in the roads and tracks. Twenty-five years ago I made a suggestion to do away with them. The public doesn't see them, and I do not see any reason for them. I wish there were a way to keep the steeple-chase and cross-country without roads and tracks. As I have said, I experimented with this at Lexington for two years, and the results were very convincing. I should say that I know it is not practical. Only a very few facilities like Lexington and Luhmuhlen would be able to do it, but everyone is entitled to a fantasy, and that is mine.

As an interesting remark, the experimental competition at Lexington brought some facts to light regarding the temperatures of horses before and after the cross-country. Before, they averaged 102 to 103 degrees. At the end of cross-country, they averaged 103 to 105 degrees. One horse, Royal Jester, went up to 107.7 degrees after cross-country and took 30 minutes to come down to 106 degrees. That was an exception. In a full-scale CCI three-star or four-star, and depending on the weather conditions, horses come back from cross-country with temperatures going from 103 to 107 plus degrees, a marked increase. As we are engaged in developing the short format, my guess would be that the difference between the experimental competition at Lexington and the actual short format will be even greater without a steeplechase anymore.

CHOOSING THE RIGHT ROUTE

Only years will tell which direction the sport is going to settle in, but we are going toward cross-country without steeplechase and roads and tracks, and there is little chance of changing that, and if you keep expending energy fighting to go back you will miss the boat.

It is far more interesting to me to work on the existing formula and get that right with the key being to find the right ratio and adapt the number of fences to the length of the course. The tendency at the moment is to have lots of jumps within a short distance. I think this is a dangerous route. You end up with a Derby course over fixed fences, and we should not make our horses victims of television or the public. Not only is it taxing on them physically, but it is also mentally unfair.

The very good riders adjusted quickly to the new format. Some are still concerned about warmup before cross-country, but all it is really, is good old horse trials that we have done all our lives.

Regarding the dressage, I say again, the quality of the tests are very impressive and get better every day. The introduction of flying changes created some problems at first, but most people quickly figured it out. The actual level looks good to me but maybe some-day we will see freestyle on a short program. Why not?

When I wrote the rules for the World Cup, I left the door open for a freestyle test. Since I am now retired and no longer involved in deci-sions regarding the sport, I have no input as such, but I think soon you could see, at least for the World Cup, a freestyle test. In prin-ciple, such a test should include all the movements in the actual tests; they are good, and the requirements are very suitable for this level of dressage.

Of course, as for the *Kur* (a dressage freestyle test), it would require a time limit. The music is another story. I do not think it is a good idea for riders to choose their music like they do in pure dressage.

It is very expensive to do and is not necessary, at least for now. A suitable style of music could be used in the background.

The show jumping has also evolved dramatically. Gone is the philosophy of testing the freshness of the horses after cross-country with jumps that were half solid and hard to knock down, with banks, ditches, water jumps, and so on. Most courses were entirely uninteresting, small jumps, and boring for the public and the riders. There again, "tradition" has been replaced by real show-jumping courses with much higher fences designed to be more technically challenging and requiring riders to be good show jumpers. The public is happy, and so am I.

26

What It Means to Be a Coach, What It Means to Be Disciplined

One of the major qualities of a coach is the ability to work with the very different personalities of the riders. A coach cannot be wishy-washy. You have to know why you are doing something. You must establish a policy to achieve your goals and then stick with it. You will always encounter those who want to change something, but you have to stick to your guns and realize that if you change something for one person, everybody will want to change your mind when they are unhappy with the decisions made. To convince others, you have to be convinced yourself.

A coach must always be intellectually fair, honest, and always think positively. This will not prevent you from making mistakes because, let's face reality, the only ones who do not make mistakes are those who do not do anything.

The coach has to realize that the stresses of trying to make the team, the struggles along the way, the highs of a successful competition, the disappointments of a perceived failure are all things that make people say and do things that they would not say or do normally. The coach has to take all of that passion and channel it into positive thinking. Focus on success. Every hardship provides an opportunity to learn. Nothing is more humbling than the horse. One moment you can be riding the wave of success, and the next, you can be sitting on the ground in the water wondering what hit you.

Understanding your riders and having that innate feeling for what will work with one, but not with another, is crucial to a coach. Some you have to treat with more consideration and handle gently. The trick is determining what will work best with each one. Today, it is called sports psychology. In 1992, when I coached the Canadian Team at Barcelona, the Canadian Federation sent a specialist to work with the Team, and we discussed the whole subject of sports psychology. He told me that it was what I was already practicing without realizing it.

The coach must be both a long-range and a short-range planner. Long-range plans include the search for raw young talent and then making them into riders who will be competitive team candidates. Bruce Davidson, Tad Coffin, David O'Connor, and others came to the team this way. I saw them competing when they were at the Preliminary Level, but I didn't care if they won or not; I was more focused on their way of riding.

On Discipline

A journalist once asked me, "What does a coach actually do?" My answer, "Basically, a coach makes you do what you do not want to do on your own."

Many factors contribute to a successful performance, but I believe one of the most vital is discipline, and above all, self-discipline. In my opinion, it is the major foundation stone for every success story in competition today and without discipline, you will be left behind. One of the foremost responsibilities of a coach is to instill discipline into an athlete, in my case riders, and make them value this quality for themselves.

Self-discipline is at the core of every athlete's success. It was the reason Muhammad Ali was a champion for so long. It is the basis of Roger Federer's success in winning both Wimbledon and the US Open in the same year at just 23 years of age and what put him on track to challenge the records of tennis legends Bjorn Borg and Pete Sampras. Think of the hours they have spent in the gym. Think of the hours Ali spent hitting a punching bag and Roger spends hitting a tennis ball.

In the case of riders, it takes discipline to train their horses on a daily basis. Oh, it might be raining, and it would be easier to stay in bed on an odd day, but trust me on this one, a missed day *will* result in a sub-standard performance. Horses thrive on a consistent, daily regime of training and so do their riders. It is the coach's job to explain this to the rider and insist on the routine being adhered to until it becomes so ingrained in the rider's mind that nothing can shake him from his goals.

From a military point of view, discipline is often seen as the ability to obey orders, a "Yes sir" or "No sir" type of response. The kind of discipline I am interested in is the discipline of work, the discipline of organization in your work, the discipline of being on time, and the discipline of meeting deadlines with an accurate and complete work product in hand. If you go to a competition you have to get your tack clean and ready, your papers have to be in order, and *you have to have the answers correct.*

Self-discipline is needed in all we do. If you take a riding lesson, you must have the discipline to pay constant attention to what you are being told and to act upon it. Fortunately, I rarely had a problem with that in my career, probably because people knew that I wouldn't put up with it.

There is also the discipline of organization. This is more where the problem tends to be. You know people are supposed to do certain things, such as learning the rules, but many times they don't. I was a dragon about this.

Too many times in my life, I have seen a competition lost by stupidity, meaning the people did not know the rules very well. They made an error. They didn't use their heads. That is unforgivable. I kept saying, and I still do, you would not conceive of a basketball player getting on the court without knowing the rules.

This equestrian sport of three-day eventing is complex because you are dealing with three different disciplines, each with separate requirements. To make it even more complicated, the FEI keeps changing the rules. Furthermore, when you go from one country to the next, national rules vary a bit. For example, the United States' rules are a little bit different from the international FEI rules, not much, but just enough to get confused. That is why I was unyielding about the riders knowing the rules and feeling comfortable with them, so that in the middle of competition they would know what to do if they got in trouble. As long as you don't get in trouble, it is pretty simple. It is when you start having a problem, and you don't know how to resolve it, that trouble starts.

I have seen even top riders getting in trouble and not know how to get out of it, and that can sink the team if you are a member. For example, if you have a refusal in the middle of a combination, and you have not studied the different ways to get out of that combination legally, you can completely mess up the team's chances. So that is the kind of discipline I really think is important. You have to do some paperwork—riders are not too keen on paperwork—which means filling out your entry forms correctly and sending them in on the right day. Sometimes the more successful riders become, the less careful they are about these things; they think they can get away with it because the organizers want to have them at their event and will overlook the riders' mistakes. Avoid this attitude at all costs because it is selfish and it is arrogant. Organizers have enough work to do, with little financial reward, without having to become a rider's administrative assistant.

Competition is becoming tougher and will continue to get tougher. These days you have got to be really sharp. It is harder to win today than it was five years ago and tougher than it was ten years ago. There are more top competitions in the world than there used to be with more top riders and horses competing in every one of them. So you can't goof off if you want to be on top.

In every competition we now have several horses getting clear rounds with no jumping penalties or time faults in cross-country and show jumping. So what makes the difference? That darned dressage! I have never yet seen a rider and a horse get 10–10–10–10 in dressage. That hasn't happened, and I don't think it will happen. Which means it doesn't matter whether you are second, third, or tenth. What counts are points. If you are 10 points from the lead after dressage, you will have to have some luck going clear in the cross-country and show jumping and hope for bad luck for the guys ahead of you because 10 points are hard to make up.

I have noticed in the United States that everybody likes to give clinics because it makes good money, and everyone likes to go to clinics because they can say, "I have been to a clinic with so-and-so." And that is all fine and dandy. But nine clinics out of ten forget about dressage. They rely on show jumping or cross-country. Nobody wants to teach dressage. Why?

Because dressage is hard and requires a lot of self-discipline on the part of both the rider and the trainer! In most clinics, you want to make money and to do that you need to have as many participants as possible, so that means the classes will be big ones. If you have six people in a dressage class, you are not going to achieve anything much in an hour-and-a-half. Every horse is a little different and every rider is different. To put those people together in a class at that level is very difficult. So what happens is you just don't do it. You skip it.

Over the years I have taught many brilliant riders, but the ones who succeed are not necessarily the most talented, they are those who pay constant attention to what is taught and then have the discipline to act upon it. When teaching, I demanded 100 percent from the rider, and nothing less.

One of the problems with eventing in the United States, and one that reflects the current American philosophy is, "We want IT now—whatever IT might be!" But there is no instant dressage like instant coffee. You can go out and buy a top-level horse if you have enough money, but the true rider should be able to "make" his or her own horse. A true rider is like a mechanic and a pilot. Some riders are mechanics, and some are pilots. The real rider can fly and take care of the engine too! These are the qualities a coach is looking for in his student.

DISCIPLINE OUT OF THE SADDLE

The successful rider must have the discipline to maintain a healthy fitness regime. Contrary to what many people believe, the rider does not "leave everything to the horse" and personal fitness is tested every time a rider gets on a horse. To the untrained eye, it may look very easy, and it may look "like the horse does all the work" but I can assure you that a great many muscles in the rider's body are being used to achieve the desired result. Being overweight works against the rider—the rounder and fuller the thighs the easier it is to fall off the horse when things go wrong.

At home in the United States, the riders were kept very active in their day-to-day lives. There were as many as six and seven horses to ride every day. This and general stable duties gave them plenty of physical exercise. The main problems arose when the team members had to go to other countries to get ready for a major competition. Often the horses had to be abroad for two and three months before the competition because of quarantine, and in the case of the Munich Olympic Games, six months of quarantine in Europe was required. It was then that the riders' fitness and weight became an issue. To deal with this, I would prepare a program for the riders as well as the horses. Sometimes we were lucky to be training near racing stables, and I would make arrangements for the riders to go and gallop two sets of horses, which helped considerably because galloping race horses is a very physically demanding activity.

At other times, they had to put on their sweat suits and go running. Stepping on the scales once a week was also required. Again, this did nothing for my popularity rating.

I ran into the biggest problems when we traveled to France, my old country, to train for the Fontainebleau Alternative Olympics in 1980. The gastronomic delights of France had adverse repercussions on my training schedule as far as the riders went. The training plan called each horse to be jogged up in front of me most mornings before the ridden sessions began which enabled me to keep an eye on the horses' soundness and to spot any problems early. As the riders jogged their horses away, I could see without any doubt the gradual enlarging of some of the riders' seats. This was especially difficult for the ladies as the fashion trend of the day was to ride in a 16-inch saddle, and if something wasn't done about it, new tack would be needed! The alarm bells sounded, and a strict regimen of running established. In spite of the screams of protest and the pleas of one gentleman, "I can't run, it makes my calves so big I can't get my boots on!" the coach persisted. I claim to this day that we had one of the leanest and fittest teams ever to set foot in a stirrup.

THE DISCIPLINE OF RIDING ON A TEAM
Riding on a team is an entirely different experience from riding as an individual. You have to put all aspirations of personal glory aside and follow instructions given by the coach to ensure that all four

team horses come safely through at the end of the day. This might mean that as first out you are given the job of pathfinder, the one to test how the course is riding. The second rider out is usually the least experienced who will benefit from the input of the pathfinder and will go for a steady clear. All pressure is on the third horse and rider to go clear and within the time if possible, and this is even more important if either of the first two riders experienced a problem. The fourth rider, if all others are home clear and sound, can go for a little bit more regarding taking all the direct routes and going for time. If one of the first three riders was retired or eliminated or the horse suffered an injury, then the pressure is on the fourth rider to complete. The rider must obey directions to the letter in order to come home safe and clear and consequently keep the team in the competition. In the 10-minute box (or now with the short format, right before the start of cross-country) the rider must listen to the coach. The coach will have been receiving reports of how the course is riding or has watched it on the close-circuit television. He knows what fence is causing which problems and will have devised a plan for dealing with some of those problems. It is imperative that the rider pays attention as it can mean the difference between success and failure for the team.

As I have said before (and I believe it might be helpful to some riders to hear it again) one of the hallmarks of my training was my insistence on the correct position of the rider and a deep, deep seat because form is function. To achieve this, I made myself extremely unpopular with many of today's top international riders. I insisted that the riders who came to me at the team headquarters spend hours in the saddle trotting on the longe line without stirrups, and on as many different horses as we could find, just as I had done at the Cadre Noir.

I was reminded of some of the creative thinking that this inspired in my students when I was inducted into the USEA Eventing Hall of Fame at the inaugural gala in 1999. One of my last resident riders, David O'Connor, very graciously made the presentation. David explained to the audience the effect that the long hours of doing sitting trot had had on both him and Bruce Davidson, one of his predecessors in the resident rider program. I sat back listening with great pride to the stories of these young men, waiting, or rather hoping, that I might hear them say I had contributed in some small way to their outstanding success in Olympic and World Championship competition over the years. But no! The audience burst into laughter upon hearing that Bruce had resorted to sewing baby diapers into his breeches, and David had bribed the lady grooms to buy him pantyhose, all in an attempt to ease their suffering and make the long hours of sitting trot more bearable. During my acceptance speech, I was able to explain that it is a well-known fact that the brains of most event riders are situated in the area of the seat and that the sitting trot is the best technique I know for moving the thinking process from the derrière up to the head, where it more properly resides.

I can almost guarantee that David is now teaching his students the very same way, and so I can take some consolation in the fact that my years as a coach were not in vain.

Coaches will not always be popular for the very simple reason that they make you do what you do not want to do. Being a successful coach in any sport, not just eventing, is not based on a popularity contest; it is based on making you do sheer hard work. Things like getting up on cold winter mornings to condition your horse when you would rather stay in bed, or spending hours trotting 20-meter circles without stirrups when you would rather go for a gentle ride in the country. The coach who is looking to be popular will not produce the desired results. The rider who does not accept discipline may be better suited to another pursuit—crochet comes to mind!

A SONG BY, TO, AND ABOUT THE RIDERS WHO TRAINED WITH JACK LE GOFF OVER THE YEARS

Sung to the Tune of "The Battle Hymn of the Republic"

Your butts have felt the torture of the training of Le Goff

Makes his riders grow as tough as nails though once they were so soft

He has made you keep your leg ON, never lets you take LEG OFF

It's you we're singing of!

CHORUS
Here's to Jack, the Gallic dragon
Keeps our spirits high, not saggin'
Now to him we'll raise a flagon
This frog we've come to love.

He is fierce and pure as brandy, brooks no shortcuts in your tack

He's been known to hurt your feelings with a true but painful crack:

"Tell me, what's that abscess I see on your horse's back?"

It's YOU he's talking of!

CHORUS
Here's to Jack, the Gallic dragon
Keeps our spirits high, not saggin'
Now to him we'll raise a flagon
This frog we've come to love.

Tad and Mike and Beth and Denny, Caroline and Ralph the Pink

Jimmy, Mary Ann and Karen, Torrance, Derek, Bruce, and Grant

David, Courtney, Holly, Cindy, Nancy, Robin and the rest:

It's them we're singing of!

CHORUS
Here's to Jack, the Gallic dragon
Keeps our spirits high, not saggin'
Now to him we'll raise a flagon
This frog we've come to love.

He has filled his teams with spirit, never thinks about defeat

If your riding isn't perfect, you will hear him oft repeat

"Get your fanny IN the saddle—don't sit on the toilet seat!"

It's Jack we're singing of!

CHORUS
Here's to Jack, the Gallic dragon
Keeps our spirits high, not saggin'
Now to him we'll raise a flagon
This frog we've come to love.

AFTERWORD

RETIREMENT, THIS TIME FOR GOOD

In 2003, I officially retired as an FEI "O" judge. My first FEI judging assignment at Wylie for Lord and Lady Hugh Russell had been back in 1974! I guess it was time to go. Because I was putting together the new FEI Eventing World Cup with some other good friends and was serving on that committee, the FEI gave me an extension so I could judge the first final of the World Cup held at Pau, France in September 2003. It was not only an honor but it also brought me great satisfaction to have my last presidency be at the first final of the Eventing World Cup.

A retirement ceremony was held on the show-jumping day. A hole was dug at the foot of the flagpole; a speech was made in French and English and my bowler hat was buried. I have to confess that I watched with a mixture of pride, sadness, and some relief.

In January 2004 Susan and I, along with our good friend Laura Field, traveled to Los Angeles where the USEF honored me with the 2003 USA Equestrian Lifetime Achievement Award for the Jimmy A. Williams Trophy. My daughter, Florence, flew in for the presentation, which meant a great deal to me. I got to wear the sterling silver hat (a replica of that worn by the great Jimmy Williams) and was proud to be among recipients that included horsemen such as William C. Steinkraus, Frank Chapot, and HRH Prince Philip, the Duke of Edinburgh.

Susan and I have been privileged to travel to some beautiful places and visit the homes of some of the most respected and generous people in the international sport of eventing. My final USEF judging assignment was at the 2005 Virginia Horse Trials in Lexington, Virginia where Penny and Brian Ross and the many riders in attendance gave me a rousing send off with that best of all gifts, a bottle of champagne. It was a good farewell!

And now I can only repeat what I said in Los Angeles at the end of my acceptance speech on that memorable evening:

"You start as a rider, then you become an instructor and coach. Then you become a judge, and then you give seminars. Then you are on the Jury of Appeals; then you get awards. And finally, the worms eat you by the feet. I think I am in the stage before the last one. But by God, if I had the chance, I would do it all over again."

Jack Le Goff
Saumur 2005

APPENDIX 1

THE CIRCLE OF CHAMPIONS

During my career I have been intimately involved with top class champions, Olympic Games individual and gold medalists, Pan-American individual gold medal lists, and, of course, other top competitors who have contributed to the teams' gold medals in Olympic, World, and Pan-American championships.

I will not take into consideration other top international competitions as it would be too involved and possibly tedious. What I am going to do is talk about those individual champions, their background, their personalities, their achievements and what has become of them at the time of this writing.

First, let's examine what we have to deal with in our sport, nay all equestrian sports. What is different about eventing is that it consists of two elements, a rider, and a horse. That is what makes it fascinating but also very challenging and frequently frustrating. Often people ask me, who of the two is the most important? The answer is, if only one of the two elements is very good, it is not going to work and the pair will not make it to the top. A very good rider on a mediocre horse cannot win, and vice versa, a mediocre rider on a very good horse cannot consistently win in top competition.

At the end of the day, on a long-term basis, the rider is the most valuable element of the two because a rider will last longer than a horse. He can ride several horses, and if he is very good, he will help the horse perform just a bit better than the horse's potential. On the other hand, the horse can help a rider reach the top level, but in a more sporadic way, which will only last for the life of the horse. At the international level, we have all known these type of riders; they become famous because they have a talented horse and win at a major competition and then we never hear from them again. In other words, at a big competition both elements of the combination of horse and rider have to be good, but in the long run, I will take the good rider.

Many times I have asked myself the question: How much time does it take to make an international horse and how much time does it take to make a rider? Well, to me, it takes about the same amount of time. It takes me three to four years to train a young horse (four or five years old) to perform at the international level. If, for comparison purposes, you get a young, reasonably talented rider, who does have some riding experience, but not much competitive experience, it will take me about three to four years to bring this rider along to the international level. Remember, I am talking about Olympic, World, and Pan-American Games level.

Once the foundation of their education has been completed by the "trainer," of course, that does not mean that the horse and rider are a finished "product." They are just ready and able to compete at that level. It is only then that their talent and determination will shape their personality. They will need continuing professional, qualified help, but at that stage, it will be more what I call "coaching."

The training of a champion requires a tremendous dedication, perseverance, and an uncompromising attitude that could all be summed up in one word: discipline. None of this is conceivable unless the trainer and coach can transmit to his students all of those principles. He achieves this by applying to himself the same work ethic and discipline that he expects from his pupils. I am convinced that becoming a champion takes a sound education in classical riding because there is a real link between the different disciplines of dressage, show jumping, and eventing. A solid knowledge of dressage is a must, especially these days, and the best show-jumping competitors in the world take lessons from top-class dressage trainers.

Eventing is very much like any other sport in the sense of discipline. Attaining excellence is a strenuous job, requiring consistent repetition day after day. Ballet dancers work on the barre daily, ice skaters carve endless circles with their blades, gymnasts work on strength, control, and coordination daily. When the schedule calls for dressage, you work on the different movements required in the test. You do it over and over again, to come as close as possible to the perfection of that particular movement. At some point, after working on these movements individually, your horse and rider will be ready to put it together to perform a dressage test in the same way a skater has to perfect the particular jumps and spins individually then put them together when performing his routine. The principle of consistent and methodical training always applies.

On the other hand, in eventing you not only have to work with the two elements of the rider and the horse, but you also have to train both to become as good as their talent (and yours) allows in three different phases: dressage, cross-country jumping, and show jumping. Here the talent of a successful trainer resides in his ability to balance all these different aspects of the sport in bringing the horse and rider to their peak at the right time.

To this already involved training schedule, a champion rider must learn horsemanship. Riders need to know how to bandage a horse for different purposes: stabling wraps, shipping wraps for traveling by van or by plane, and the delicate bandaging required for galloping and competition. They also have to learn about nutrition, basic veterinary care, and the most vital part of the event horse—the legs. They should know what sound or healthy legs look like and how they feel. You will know if riders have achieved this when you blind-fold them, and they can tell which horse it is by feeling the legs. I could do it with my horses and so can they.

Shoeing is also a large part of the equation. You do not expect the rider to shoe his horse, but he should know enough about it to tell a farrier what he expects of him. In other words, a champion will know and be aware of every detail of caring for his horse properly, even to the point of keeping his horse safe. These aspects of horsemanship are learned on a daily basis as the sched-ule in the stable follows an organized plan. As I have said elsewhere in this book, there is no instant horsemanship and no instant top-class rider.

I will now introduce you to some of the riders I have had the pleasure to train and coach, and I will share with you some of the characteristics that made them champions in their own right.

THE INDIVIDUAL CHAMPIONS (LISTED CHRONOLOGICALLY)

JEAN-JACQUES GUYON

Individual gold medalist, Mexico Olympics, 1968.

Jean-Jacques began his riding career in Saumur as a member of the Cadre Noir and as such had a thorough equestrian education. He had been focus-ing on dressage and was a member of the high school quadrille as well as the Sauteurs (the unit that performs the airs about the ground). As with most members of the Cadre Noir, he had also been steeplechasing, show jumping, and eventing. Consequently, when Jean-Jacques came to me to train with the French squad in Fontainebleau, I did not have to teach him how to ride. Although a bit younger than me, he had the same background, so I understood him very well. What I had to do with him was make him a fighter, a winner. I do not know if it was a lack of ambition, or that he did not have a naturally aggressive personality, but he did not have what I call "the killer instinct."

Jean-Jacques was a very pleasant gentleman who liked to keep to himself. He was rarely exuberant but was very conscientious, intelligent, capable of analyzing a situation, dependable and therefore made an excellent team member. With his horse Pitou, Jean-Jacques placed fourth in the European Championships held in Ireland the year before the Mexico Olympics, so his gold medal was not a fluke as they had shown some good form. Although he was one of the riders who had the good fortune to ride cross-country before the infamous storm in Mexico, he would nevertheless have finished in the top placing, storm or no storm. Of course, I had to train him and his horse to per-fect their technique, but that was rather easy, as I did not have to teach him how to ride but just make the combination of horse and rider sharper; in other words, I improved, rather than corrected, his way of riding. I had to make him believe that he was better than he thought he was.

After Mexico, Jean-Jacques left the army for a career in the civilian equestrian world. He was not made for that, and it did not suit his temperament. He had some good opportunities like being in charge of all equestrian aspects of Club Med. I am sure he did a good job, but I doubt that he was happy. He probably would have been better off staying in the army where he would have had a decent career as an officer.

BRUCE DAVIDSON

Back-to-back individual World Champion 1974 and 1978. Pan Am individual gold and team gold medalist, 1995. Olympic team gold, 1976, 1984, team silver 1972, 1996.

I first saw Bruce at Neil Ayer's Ledyard Farm in Wenham, Massachusetts, in the spring of 1970 at a "round-up" of young riders that I had asked Meg Plumb to organize. It was essential to identify those young riders who had an interest in becoming part of a US Equestrian Team Young Riders Program with the ultimate goal of becoming a team rider.

Bruce was then an attractive 19-year-old young man with a lean athletic look. Although I could see that his riding was not polished, his concentration and general attitude gave me a good feeling, and I invited him, along with several others, to come to the headquarters of the USET in Gladstone, New Jersey, to ride in a training session and undergo further evaluation.

During the training session it became apparent to me that I was working with raw talent. Bruce only needed to be educated about classical riding and technically trained to compete. In fact, Bruce did not have much experience in riding and little, if any, in real competition. He had been in boarding school in Maryland and was a member of the school's equestrian program headed by Mr. Patrick Lynch (soon to become USET Farm Manager). Bruce had also spent a short time in Ireland with Iris Kellet, and this was about the total of his riding background.

I invited him to stay and train with the team along with a couple of other riders, including the two Powers brothers, one of whom became the reserve rider for the Munich Olympic Games two years later. The training started in early summer, and I could clearly see the progress that Bruce was making with each passing day.

As the United States only had three active, experienced Team riders at this time, I knew that to be successful in Munich we would need some of these young riders ready to complete a team and be competitive, and I had just two short years to accomplish this.

I pushed them very hard every day for over two years. I knew I was very demanding, and a hell of a tough coach, and I would not have won any prizes in a popularity contest, but they all put up with it. Bruce was no exception. I kept the pressure on him and the others, and I could not have blamed them if they had killed me in a dark corner if they had had the chance.

Few riders have natural talent and feeling, but Bruce was one of the chosen few. He had an amazing ability to learn and his power of concentration and his physical strength helped him a great deal. The daily schedule was hard, starting with stable work, mucking out, grooming, cleaning the entire stable, then getting ready for riding lessons. Contrary to Jean-Jacques Guyon who had a solid background in classical riding before training for the French Olympic Team, Bruce had little knowledge of dressage, show jumping, and cross-country so I had to teach him how to ride first. The longe line was part of the training, of course, then came the position, the use of the aids, and on and on. Thanks to the USET I had some team horses for these young riders to ride and that was a significant factor in the upbringing of these potential champions. Bruce's parents acquired Irish Cap (see p. 58), but he was very green and had to be trained to become an international horse, just like Bruce had to be trained to become an international rider. Cappy was a great addition to the barn and with the string of horses we now had, I could start to make something of these young riders.

I used the local horse shows and dressage competitions to give both horses and riders the necessary mileage in public. We were not chasing the ribbons, just the experience. Bruce was very organized, always clean and properly dressed, and his horses were turned out to a high standard. This attention to detail and his ability to learn made him an excellent student and very easy to teach.

After some successful competitions in the US Bruce was selected for the team traveling to in Munich. We had to leave early and train in England, and I know it was a hard six months for both him and Jim Powers who had also been short-listed, but it did these two young men a world of good to be in England and ride against some of the top international riders in the world. Not only did they compete against the British, but many other foreign riders were training and competing there, and it was an invaluable experience and gave them both a feel for what to expect in Munich.

In Munich, Bruce joined the team of Mike Plumb, Kevin Freeman, and Jim Wofford and rode the team horse, Plain Sailing. Jim Powers was the reserve rider. The US won the silver medal, and Bruce contributed to this more than honorable result.

Two years later, riding Irish Cap (who had matured nicely), Bruce won the first of his two World Championships. I can still visualize Irish Cap and Bruce landing down a severe drop on the cross-country course. I would say that Bruce saved the horse from falling. He not only stayed firmly in the saddle but his efforts stopped Cappy from rolling. Nine riders out of ten would have had a fall, but I suppose that is what makes the difference between a good rider and a championship title holder. Bruce thoroughly earned the title of champion that day.

It gave me great pleasure in those days to watch him ride cross-country using all his dressage training to lengthen the stride when required and shorten it as necessary in a smooth and barely noticeable manner. He gave a textbook display of how you should ride across the country and make the time—asking the horse to come back to him without ever fighting him. Irish Cap and Bruce were the complete expression of my teaching philosophy that day.

Oh, everything was not rosy all of the time. One of the technical aspects I had to work hard on was the show jumping. Bruce was always leaning on the same side over the jumps and consequently the horses always landed on the same lead. That took a while to correct.

Bruce loved his horses, but at times he did not think, nor accept, that there could be something wrong with them. Like all the team riders, Bruce was on his own at home after the season ended and came for training sessions in the winter and spring before the next season started. During the preparation for the 1978 World Championships in Lexington, Kentucky, Irish Cap was, unfortunately, not sound. Bruce could not accept that fact, and I had to be very forceful about not putting him on the team and instead insisting he ride Might Tango who, while short on experience, was completely sound. At the end of the day, Bruce won his second World title with Might Tango, but by that time our relationship had deteriorated and there was some tension between us. This situation did last quite a while, but it was also at a time when Bruce had some personal problems, which I am sure did not help. You have to give time to the time! Years have gone by, and Bruce is still competing. I got as much pleasure watching him ride cross-country at 60 as I did when he was 20. No matter what, one has to have respect for this man who has made the most of his horses from the ground up. Not many riders can claim that. Deep inside I feel that even at the lowest point of our relationship, something persevered, maybe something called trust. At least that is the way I feel.

TAD COFFIN

Individual and team gold medal, 1975 Pan Am Games, Mexico. Individual and team gold medal, 1976 Olympic Games, Montreal.

Event riders come in many shapes and sizes, and also come from many different backgrounds. Tad Coffin was an equitation rider, having acquired this art from a talented teacher, Raul de Leon. Tad grew up on Long Island, New York, where he competed in both equitation and hunter classes with great success. He came to me with a lovely position both on the flat and over fences. I did not have to teach him that most critical of things, the fundamental basic of riding: form is function. What I did have to teach Tad was using his position to communicate with the horses and teaching them what they needed to learn about dressage. Equitation is mostly a competition judged on the rider's position, the horses being required to do only simple basic movements. There is nothing complicated about equitation but it is a good start for a rider as he has to cultivate his position and use of aids with discretion. The same goes for the hunters: it is also a good way to learn how to jump with a good position and good balance over the fence. The rider can educate his eye regarding timing and stride. I love to have riders with this background as it is easy to go from there to show jumping, dressage, and cross-country. Tad was similar to Mike Plumb, who had also grown up in the hunter and equitation world. It is also the best way to start young horses in jumping competition. The hunter courses are flowing with accurate distances, and again it is easy to go from there and move to the jumpers or cross-country. In the United States, equitation and hunter classes can be an end in themselves. Some riders and horses specialize in doing just that. I use this type of training as a means to an end, which is eventing or show jumping.

Tad had all of that to start with; how lucky for him and how lucky for me. Tad is a purist in all its real meaning. He is dedicated, focused, and has the power of concentration, all of which are indispensable for learning and competing. He is also disciplined, organized, and polished. Wow! Here in one young man were so many of those qualities necessary to become a champion. And I think about how lucky I was to have all of those young men and women as my protégés (and victims) at the same time.

All of the riders in my circle of champions had one common denominator—intelligence. I have never yet met a champion, in any sport, and particularly in eventing, which requires a broad knowledge of riding and horsemanship, who was not an intelligent individual. Not all individual intelligent event riders will become champions, but all champions are intelligent, and Tad is certainly no exception. Often top competitions are won by the slightest margin of points, and it is more often the smart one who ends up winning by saving every point possible during those long, stressful three days involving three different disciplines. Have a look at the history of decathlon; it is a similar kind of competition.

Tad also had another weapon in his armory: he had feeling and that is one ingredient that you cannot teach. You either have it or you don't. Does it mean that you cannot be a good rider without feeling? No, I am not saying that, but the rider with little feeling will have to work harder and for a longer period to replace that lack of feeling with a systematic technique. On the other hand, during my career, I had some riders with definite feeling but who were not dedicated enough to work hard, and they did not succeed.

Tad was individual Pan Am and Olympic gold medalist at 22 years old. Where do you go from there? He kept competing for a while but also then dedicated himself to teaching and took on a big challenge in running a large equestrian operation called Flying Horse Farm in Hamilton, Massachusetts. Because Tad is a purist, he devoted a tremendous amount of time to teaching and running this establishment to the point where he ran himself into the ground through sheer hard work. It was an enormous task for one man to take on, even if that man was Tad Coffin.

After Flying Horse Farm, Tad took on another challenge, the Morven Park International Equestrian School at Morven Park in Virginia. But this time around he called on his teacher of the early days, Raul de Leon, to join him as co-director of the only equestrian riding school for instructors in the entire United States at that time. It was run much like a college, with dormitories, boarding facilities, and a cafeteria. The school owned a fair number of horses, but sadly, the tuition paid by the students was not enough to cover the expenses. Contrary to most countries where such establishments receive government support, Morven Park lacked the financial backing to keep the enterprise going indefinitely and closed its doors in 1992. The end of an era indeed, and it was the last such riding school in the United States where riders could go and learn how to ride and teach. What a shame!

Today, Tad has taken an entirely different route. He has put together a saddle-making business and has created his own way to build saddles using his own machinery. Tad and his wife are raising their four children in Virginia, and he seems to do very well for himself. He owns a plane that he flies himself. I am sure he brought to his flying all those qualities that made him such an incredible rider. I am always thrilled when he comes to visit with some of his children. What a reward for a retired coach to have his old students keep in touch and come to spend time with him.

NICK HOLMES-SMITH

Individual and team gold medalist for Canada, Pan American Games, 1991, Dalton, Georgia.

My next champion on the list is a rider I coached when the Canadians asked me to help them and brought me out of retirement as a coach. At the time, Nick was a very different type of rider; possibly more because he is a different type of person. He is a very personable kind of a guy who had traveled extensively to many places in the world and especially to New Zealand where he has built many cross-country courses. He also went to Tibet, establishing contacts with the locals. He traveled extremely light and took almost nothing with him in the way of clothing and money. I trust that our friendship will survive if I do take the plunge and say that Nick was the "gypsy of the equestrian world," always laid back, very communicative with people, and thoroughly enjoying life.

People might think that he did not look like a serious contender for international competition. Would they be right or wrong? Wrong! Nick thoroughly loved horses and their company, and he had a great rapport with them. Nick had the fortune, or misfortune, to become a good buddy with another Canadian rider, David Wilding-Davies. They were a pair. They both had plenty of talent and were blessed with superior intelligence. I am not sure what their background was before I got involved with them, so I will pass on that part. Because they were inseparable, I have to talk about both of them. Teaching them riding was the easy part of my job. The tough part was everything else apart from the riding. The stable management was not bad, not good; it did not exist. The condition of their equipment was indescribably bad, the tack, in particular, had not had much care for a long time. Their clothes and way of dressing were not much better, but with the help of some kind people, including my Susan who gave them some breeches, things gradually got better.

I have to mention an anecdote in connection with the state of their equipment. Nick and David had obtained their pilot's licenses and bought a small plane they flew themselves. (Remember, I said they were intelligent people!) One day they came to me and said, "Would you like to come with us and have some fun? We're sure you will enjoy it." While very touched by this invitation, I, without any hesitation, turned them down flat, telling them, "I have seen how you take care of your equipment, and there is no chance in Hades that you will get me on your plane unless you tie down my legs and arms!"

But in spite of all of these stories of their mismanagement of their equipment, they were dedicated to their horses and their riding beyond all else. Nick, the future Pan Am champion, had excellent riding ability in all three disciplines, though dressage was the least attractive phase to him. The horse that he rode in the Pan Ams was Ruderpest (see p. 125). He was a big gray horse with plenty of ability and was owned by Paul Popiel, brother of Trojan Horse Ranch Horse Trials organizer, Andrew Popiel. I will sum it up by saying that Nick and Ruderpest were ready for the challenge of the Pan Am Championship, and they performed exceedingly well. It was a great satisfaction to me that Nick not only won the individual gold medal but Team Canada also won the gold over Bermuda (silver) and Mexico (bronze). I had mixed feelings about it all because my ex-US Team did not have much success at these Pan Ams, but I was very proud of the Canadian riders. Nick had a lot of experience and was a particularly good jockey cross-country, even if he did get a bit loose over the jumps. He had excellent balance, which helped, and he trusted that he would be just fine, but that caught up with him at the Olympic Games in Barcelona. Riding a real ping pong ball of a little dun horse, Lancelot, Nick found himself on the ground after his horse bucked him off over a jump. Such are the humbling abilities of the horse.

I always enjoyed working with Nick, largely because he was so much fun to be around. In fact, the whole Canadian Team was always ready to party. But with maturity comes a change in your sense of values and priorities. Nick finally planted his tent in one spot in western Canada. He got married and now has quite a large family. At first, he conducted summer camps for riders and was very successful, I am told. But the demands of his growing family created a need for a more substantial and reliable income, and he ventured out into the world of helicopter skiing. He still is very involved with eventing and horses. He has built up his training center, organized events, and is a course designer. So my gypsy friend is now settled down, the head of a family and a successful businessman. And incidentally, David Wilding-Davies also got married, has children, and guess what, he is the head of a coffee plantation in Zimbabwe!

DAVID O'CONNOR

Individual gold medal and team bronze medal, 2000 Olympics, Sydney, Australia. Team gold medal, 2002 World Equestrian Games, Jerez, Spain. Individual silver medal and team gold, 1999 Pan American Games, Winnipeg, Canada.

David is a product of the young riders' program and spent four-and-a-half years with me as the last USET resident rider in Hamilton, Massachusetts. Although that was long before he won his gold medal in Sydney, I somewhat selfishly like to take a little credit for all that time he spent day in and day out with me. I soon realized that David had huge potential, and that means the grinder was turned on, and the compliments were not dispensed as profusely as the criticisms, but if I pounded hard I hope I was honest in my teaching. David was born into a family steeped in horses on his mother's side. At an early age, David's mother Sally took David and brother Brian on a trip across the United States from East coast to West coast on horseback. I guess David knows what hacking across the country means!

Before coming to the Team, David spent some time at Jimmy Wofford's stable in Virginia as a working pupil. So don't try to tell him about mucking out and mowing grass! He knows all about it, and I am sure he learned a few other things as a young rider, thanks to Jimmy.

Although David was exposed to horses and their training from a very young age, his family did not have the means to buy him an upper-level horse, so his competitive experience was rather modest. What a great opportunity that talented young riders like David, with no financial backing, could train at the team for free and be able to get competitive mileage with the few team horses that were still there. Looking at the riders that came out of that program like Bruce, Tad, David, and others, it was money well spent.

David is one who had to work hard as it did not always come easy for him, but when he got it, he really got it. His physical ability was always there, but the most important factor in his progression up to the international level was his intellectual ability to comprehend, analyze, and implement what he was learning every day. Here again, we have an intelligent individual coupled with a strong physical body and the determination to succeed. It is absolutely no coincidence that all the riders in the Circle of Champions are truly intelligent.

David's record includes some great performances like winning Badminton, being on gold-, silver-, and bronze-medal teams in championships, and winning individual Olympic gold. The list is impressive. I am exceedingly proud and happy to say I have been able to contribute to his success, but probably most proud to witness him become a great leader as well. David is not only a good teacher, team leader, and rider, but also a great ambassador for all equestrian sports.

David went on to be president of the US Equestrian Federation. He was probably the most important factor in the resolution of the long, hard, and costly dispute between the USET and the former AHSA. The United States equestrian community owes him a great deal. We try to stay in touch as much as possible. I always enjoy our encounters, or even just a phone call.

Being the president of the USEF, a member of the FEI Eventing Committee and performing multiple other functions is very commendable but it does not put the butter on the bread, so David still has to earn a living teaching, coaching, and training. It is his natural way of doing things. Do not be surprised if, when the time comes, David is appointed the next coach of the US Eventing Team. Mark my words! That would be the best thing that could happen to the US Team.

AND THE TEAM CHAMPIONS (ALPHABETICALLY)

J. MICHAEL PLUMB

Team silver medal at Tokyo Olympics in 1964, Mexico in 1968, and Munich in 1972. Team gold and individual silver medals at Montreal in 1976. Team gold medal at Los Angeles Games in 1984.

Now I will turn to the team champions, and I must first list Mike Plumb. Mike served as team captain during all the years I was the coach for the United States Equestrian Team.

Horses are what have fulfilled Mike's life. I was about to say exclusively, but I would be wrong. Mike also had an inclination toward the ladies. There is nothing wrong with that, especially when the ladies that Mike liked were good looking (well, jealousy makes you say things you really should not say!). But to be serious, Mike was totally immersed in the sport of eventing. Let's say 90 percent of his concentration was taken up with this sport.

Mike has competed on eight Olympic Teams, including the 1980 alternative Olympics in Fontainebleau, France. Truly a record in equestrian sport and must certainly be close to the Guinness Book of World Records for all sports, but he never had time for anything else like media interviews or self-promotion. I once told Mike he should consider having an agent, and his answer was, "Why don't you do it for me?" My response was, "Look, my friend, I have plenty to do to make your seat straight! Anyway, I am not an agent." Too bad because I could and would have brought Mike some fame and sponsorship. He has had a tremendous reward from his satisfaction in his accomplishments, but he is probably less known than others who have not accomplished half as much, and that is because they have known how to market themselves, which, of course, brings public exposure and financial support from advertisers and sponsors.

As a rider, you could not dream of a better captain because he was very team-oriented. I had to work hard on his position in dressage to make him sit up straight as his shoulders are a little closed, making it difficult for him to have the presence, or prestance as the French would say, in the dressage arena. But my god, he was the most accurate test rider ever to set foot in a ring, and he made a very commendable effort to work on his position.

On cross-country day there was no rider more dependable than Mike. You would see him off at the start and go to the finish line assured that Mike would get home no matter how tough the course, no matter which horse he was riding, and no matter what the conditions. I have told you about the one mistake that Mike ever made on a cross-country course and the only time he didn't get home, and I am sure he still carries that with him to this day. But you have to look at all the good work that he has done for the team. Always ready to sacrifice himself in the interests of the team: always available to help the younger riders, Mike's experience and knowledge were invaluable to me.

His background in riding was from the show ring in equitation and hunters. That gave him a solid base in jumping, balance, and timing. He was a very hard worker, never satisfied with the way his horses were going, always wanting them to go better, sometimes too much so. Many times I had to convince him to get out of the ring and take the horses for a good hack in the countryside.

Mike was also an excellent athlete. He played serious football in college and was very strong and extremely tough. He never got tired and was always on the ball. Mike still rides and teaches, which I think he finds hard to do after so many years of competition. No matter how often we had some rough times with each other, I could never hold a grudge towards Mike. He is a straight shooter, although not the best diplomat and that has not always served him well, but he is the most reliable and truest friend, and always will be.

KAREN STIVES

Individual silver medal, team gold medal, Los Angeles Olympic Games.

Karen is another talented, determined and very intelligent rider who, even though she never won a world title, contributed greatly to the US Team's medals in the top FEI Championships. She represented the United States in both World Championships and Olympic Games. Her biggest contribution was her individual silver medal in Los Angeles in 1984 just behind Mark Todd and Charisma. Riding the big, gray Ben Arthur, Karen received high marks in dressage, particularly from François Lucas, who was very impressed by the way the horse moved so fluidly and with so much power and elegance. François is not a very generous judge, so Ben Arthur and Karen had to have done a good job to deserve the high marks he gave them. Karen continued to ride brilliantly for the rest of the competition and was instrumental in clinching the team gold medal. Earlier in this book, there is a section that talks about Karen and another horse, Silent Partner, but Ben Arthur has a story all of his own. In fact, it is a story about Karen's mother, Lillian Maloney. To my knowledge, Mrs. Maloney had never been on a horse in her life, but she always came to watch Karen compete, and besides criticizing the shape of my trousers, she had a great eye for picking good horses. She is the one who chose Ben Arthur. I believe that was during the 1982 World Championships in Luhmuhlen, and just two years later, he and Karen won individual silver in the Olympics!

TORRANCE WATKINS

Individual bronze medal, Fontainebleau Alternative Olympic Games, France, 1980. Team gold, Olympic Games, Los Angeles, 1984.

During my tenure as a coach, several riders, although never winning individual championships themselves, have made a tremendous contribution to the team, helping to win the medals that made the US number one for years. Torrance Watkins is one of them.

With her talent and strength of personality, Torrance competed several times on the US Team in international championships. She was a very determined competitor and could be aggressive, so I have to include her in the "fighter" group. Torrance could be very sweet and charming, but her competitive temperament also caused her to have an unpredictable attitude at times.

236

Somehow she managed to make these unusual characteristics work to her advantage in competition.

When thinking about Torrance's contribution to the success of the team, my mind immediately conjures up the picture of her and Poltroon. This combination captured the imagination of the eventing world and also conquered it. Two particular occasions stand out. First, their second place at Burghley in 1979 where they added just 5.6-time penalties on cross-country to finish 1.6 penalties behind Andrew Hoy and Davey, and the alternative Olympic Games in Fontainebleau, France, in 1980 where they won individual bronze.

The grace, lightness, and beauty expressed by the pair in the dressage phase had all the spectators fascinated by this little "Indian" mare. It was a perfect match, and horse and rider fitted each other like a glove. The next day, watching them flying and jumping with ease around the cross-country was a real treat. This only served to attract a huge crowd who came to see this unusual but oh-so-attractive pair go brilliantly in the show jumping.

Torrance was full of talent not only as a rider but in other fields as well. She worked in the fashion industry as a model, which should be no surprise to anyone. She is a gorgeous lady with class and good taste to burn. From there she went into the fragrance industry testing different perfumes. I have a friend in this business whose name is Jean-Paul Guerlain. He is a horseman and competed for many years in dressage and driving. He is the boss of the well-known House of Guerlain perfume company. I wish I had introduced Torrance to Jean-Paul as I think they would have had so much in common.

Back to the riding: Torrance was an elegant dressage rider, polished and precise. On cross-country, she belonged to that group of ladies that "went for it." She knew no fear and would ride any horse small or big; the breed or color mattered not, as long as the horse had the talent and heart to do the job.

Torrance went on to become a successful course designer. For a few years, she and partner Erik Fleming organized the superb Over the Walls event in Hardwick, Massachusetts. She is a perfectionist, and this guaranteed the competitors a jolly good cross-country course to ride over, as well as enjoying a very special time at her events. I had the distinct pleasure of judging an FEI Eventing World Cup Qualifier there a few years ago. It was an amazing experience, and I am a great fan.

JIM WOFFORD

Olympic team silver medals at Mexico, 1968 and Munich 1972. Individual silver medal, Fontainebleau, 1980.

Jim Wofford is another rider who contributed so much to help the team bring the bacon home. Jim had already competed on the US Team before my arrival in the country. Jim, in my book, is the perfect example of a "thinker." His brain has many little drawers, each one for its own subject, and he can open those drawers in an instant. He is usually very calm and relaxed. Do not mistake me, lethargic he is not. He can shift gears at a speed of lightning, especially so in competition. Jim leaves nothing to chance. His ability to plan his schedule allows him to keep time for himself and his family, while also meeting the needs of his many students, fulfill his writing and speaking commitments, and do his utmost to promote the sport on television. If Jim has 20 minutes of free time, he can make himself go to sleep instantly and wake up exactly when the 20 minutes are up to continue with his schedule.

Faithfulness defines Jim's personality. I can testify to that. During my coaching career, I achieved a high level of satisfaction; I had fun and was almost always comfortable performing my role. However, as I have mentioned previously in this book, the last weeks leading up to the Los Angeles Olympics were some of the most daunting moments in my entire career. I will never forget the strength of Jim's support; it made him a faithful friend and a towering personality in my mind.

Our relationship was different from my relationship with all the other riders. We both like to fish and hunt, and we managed to do some of that almost every year. What was unusual was that the two friends going fishing and hunting together were two very different people from the coach and the rider when at work for the team. It was so much that way that we never talked about the team and the horses when fishing and hunting. Many times we had to call each other the day following our escapades to talk about work. It was something we both instinctively were able to do. We never had to decide to separate work from relaxation, and we were very comfortable with that arrangement.

As a rider, Jim had a good basic knowledge. As a little boy of nine or ten, he had ridden in the very first horse trials held in the United States and had been in the saddle almost all his life. He was particularly at home in the jumping and cross-country department, and it was easy for me to work with him. His power of concentration was unusual; it never wavered, even when you have to repeat different exercises many times. That was never due to lack of understanding; the points I had made in the very first lesson had been filed away in one of those little drawers in his head. No, the repetition was to help the horse understand the concepts and then to fine-tune and improve until we had both horse and rider in perfect harmony.

Jim was on many teams during my time with the team. His calm attitude and sincere cooperation were of great help to his teammates, and definitely to me. He saved some situations that could have resulted in an embarrassing moment to the riders and that could have had a disastrous effect on the team. (Those stories will have to wait for my next book.)

He is now doing multitudes of clinics sharing his years of experience and his very special intellectual talents with his students. He still enjoys fishing and hunting, and I hope that we will be able to enjoy some days together on the banks of a river very soon.

APPENDIX 2

LIFETIME ACHIEVEMENT RECORD OF JACK LE GOFF

OFFICIAL SERVICE

FEI Official Eventing Judge

USEF Eventing Judge "R"

FEI Three-Day Eventing Committee

COMPETITIVE ACHIEVEMENTS

Three-Day French National Champion 1956 and 1964

French Olympic Three-Day Team Member 1960 (Bronze Team Medal) and 1964

PROFESSIONAL BACKGROUND AND MAJOR COACHING ACCOMPLISHMENTS

Cadre Noir, Saumur, France: Riding Master 1952–1961

**French Equestrian Federation, Fontainebleau, France
Head Coach and Trainer (1965–1968)**

1967 European Junior Championships: Three-Day Team Gold, Individual Gold and Bronze Medals, Eridge, England

1968 Mexico Olympic Games: Individual Gold Medal Winner

1968 European Junior Championships: Three-Day Team Gold, Individual Silver and Bronze Medals, Craon, France

United States Equestrian Team Head Coach and Trainer

1972 Munich Olympic Games: Team Silver Medal

1974 World Championships, Britain: Team Gold Medal, Individual Gold and Silver Medals

1975 Pan American Games, Mexico: Team Gold Medal, Individual Gold and Silver Medals

1976 Montreal Olympic Games: Team Gold Medal, Individual Gold and Silver Medals

1978 World Championships, United States: Team Bronze Medal, Individual Gold Medal

1980 Alternate Olympic Games, France: Individual Silver and Bronze Medals

1982 World Championships, Germany: Team Bronze Medal, Individual Bronze Medal

1984 Los Angeles Olympic Games: Team Gold Medal, Individual Silver Medal

Director USET Training Center 1985–1992

Canadian Equestrian Team Head Coach and Trainer 1990–1992

1990 Stockholm World Equestrian Games

1991 Pan American Championships: Team Gold Medal, Individual Gold Medal

1992 Barcelona Olympic Games: Fielded team for competition

INTERNATIONAL JUDGING RECORD

1994   Ground Jury Member — World Equestrian Games, The Hague, Holland

1995   Ground Jury President — European Championships, Pratoni Del Vivaro, Italy

1996   Ground Jury Member — Atlanta Olympic Games, Georgia, United States

1997   Ground Jury President — European Championships, Burghley, England

1999   Ground Jury President — European Young Riders Championships, Ireland

2000   Ground Jury President — European Junior Championships, Pratoni Del Vivaro, Italy

2000   Jury of Appeal Member — Sydney Olympics, Sydney, Australia

2003   Ground Jury President — FEI Eventing World Cup Final, Pau, France

Judged every major three-day event in the world

CAREER RECOGNITION

1983   USEF Horseman of the Year, United States

1983   USEA Wofford Trophy, United States

1999   USEA Hall of Fame

2004   USEF Lifetime Achievement Award, Jimmy Williams Trophy

FEI EVENTING WORLD CUP

2002   Created the FEI Eventing World Cup and chaired the committee charged with its development

APPENDIX 3

DEVELOPMENT OF THE OLYMPIC EVENTING FORMAT

1912, Stockholm, Sweden: Called the "Pentathlon on Horseback" or "Military," this was the forerunner of the Three-Day Event. It consisted of five trials or phases:

1. A Long distance ride of 34.5 miles (55km).
2. A Cross-country of 3.125 miles (5km).
3. A Steeplechase of 2.2 miles (3.5km).
4. Prize jumping.
5. Prize riding (dressage).

The event was open to officers riding military horses and the minimum weight to be carried was 182 pounds (80kg).

1920 Antwerp, Belgium: The second Military was run in 1920. Interestingly there was no dressage phase held at this Olympic Games. Antwerp saw the introduction of bonus points that could be earned by the riders.

1924 Paris, France: The format was established that would hold with minor changes until 2004 when the "short format" was introduced. In 1924, dressage moved to the first day of competition; speed and endurance took place on the second day, and jumping on the third.

The speed and endurance consisted of five phases:

A) Roads and Tracks of 4.9 miles (7.84km).
B) Steeplechase of 2.5 miles (4km).
C) Roads and Tracks of 9 miles (14.4km).
D) Cross-country of 5.5 miles (8.8 km).
E) Run-in of 1.25 miles (2km).

Fence dimensions were a maximum of 3 feet, 11 inches high and 13 feet wide.

The Phase A Roads and Tracks, completed mostly at the trot with some walk or canter included, served as a warm-up for Phase B Steeplechase, and Phase C as a cool-down to give the horse a breather before cross-country.

1966 World Championships, Burghley, Great Britain: Phase E was dropped from the Three-Day Event format.

1969: The compulsory 10-minute "vet box" at the end of Phase C was introduced. This allowed the horses to be inspected by a veterinarian: their temperatures, pulses, respiration, and soundness were checked.

2004: The Olympic Games became a "short format" competition with phases A, B, and C being eliminated.

INDEX

HORSES CAME FIRST, SECOND, AND LAST